LANGUAGE AND LITERACY SERIES

Dorothy S. Strickland, Fou[...]
Celia Genishi and Donna E. Alver[...]
ADVISORY BOARD: *Richard Allington, Kathryn Au[...]*
Anne Haas Dyson, Carole Edelsky, Mary Juzwik, Susa[...]

Every Young Child a Reader: Using Marie Clay's
Key Concepts for Classroom Instruction
SHARAN A. GIBSON AND BARBARA MOSS

"You Gotta BE the Book": Teaching Engaged and
Reflective Reading with Adolescents, Third Edition
JEFFREY D. WILHELM

Personal Narrative, Revised:
Writing Love and Agency in the High School Classroom
BRONWYN CLARE LAMAY

Inclusive Literacy Teaching: Differentiating Approaches in
Multilingual Elementary Classrooms
LORI HELMAN, CARRIE ROGERS, AMY FREDERICK, & MAGGIE STRUCK

The Vocabulary Book:
Learning and Instruction, Second Edition
MICHAEL F. GRAVES

Reading, Writing, and Talk: Inclusive Teaching Strategies
for Diverse Learners, K–2
MARIANA SOUTO-MANNING & JESSICA MARTELL

Go Be a Writer!: Expanding the Curricular Boundaries of
Literacy Learning with Children
CANDACE R. KUBY & TARA GUTSHALL RUCKER

Partnering with Immigrant Communities:
Action Through Literacy
GERALD CAMPANO, MARÍA PAULA GHISO, & BETHANY J. WELCH

Teaching Outside the Box but Inside the Standards:
Making Room for Dialogue
BOB FECHO, MICHELLE FALTER, & XIAOLI HONG, EDS.

Literacy Leadership in Changing Schools:
10 Keys to Successful Professional Development
SHELLEY B. WEPNER, DIANE W. GÓMEZ, KATIE EGAN CUNNINGHAM,
KRISTIN N. RAINVILLE, & COURTNEY KELLY

Literacy Theory as Practice:
Connecting Theory and Instruction in K–12 Classrooms
LARA J. HANDSFIELD

Literacy and History in Action: Immersive Approaches to
Disciplinary Thinking, Grades 5–12
THOMAS M. MCCANN, REBECCA D'ANGELO, NANCY GALAS,
& MARY GRESKA

Pose, Wobble, Flow:
A Culturally Proactive Approach to Literacy Instruction
ANTERO GARCIA & CINDY O'DONNELL-ALLEN

Newsworthy—Cultivating Critical Thinkers, Readers, and
Writers in Language Arts Classrooms
ED MADISON

Engaging Writers with Multigenre Research Projects:
A Teacher's Guide
NANCY MACK

Teaching Transnational Youth—
Literacy and Education in a Changing World
ALLISON SKERRETT

Uncommonly Good Ideas—
Teaching Writing in the Common Core Era
SANDRA MURPHY & MARY ANN SMITH

The [...]
Work [...]
JENN[...]

Critical Encounters in Secondary English:
Teaching Literary Theory to Adolescents, Third Edition
DEBORAH APPLEMAN

Transforming Talk into Text—Argument Writing, Inquiry,
and Discussion, Grades 6–12
THOMAS M. MCCANN

Reading and Representing Across the Content Areas:
A Classroom Guide
AMY ALEXANDRA WILSON & KATHRYN J. CHAVEZ

Writing and Teaching to Change the World:
Connecting with Our Most Vulnerable Students
STEPHANIE JONES, ED.

Educating Literacy Teachers Online:
Tools, Techniques, and Transformations
LANE W. CLARKE & SUSAN WATTS-TAFFEE

Other People's English: Code-Meshing,
Code-Switching, and African American Literacy
VERSHAWN ASHANTI YOUNG, RUSTY BARRETT,
Y'SHANDA YOUNG-RIVERA, & KIM BRIAN LOVEJOY

WHAM! Teaching with Graphic Novels Across
the Curriculum
WILLIAM G. BROZO, GARY MOORMAN, & CARLA K. MEYER

The Administration and Supervision of Reading Programs,
5th Edition
SHELLEY B. WEPNER, DOROTHY S. STRICKLAND,
& DIANA J. QUATROCHE, EDS.

Critical Literacy in the Early Childhood Classroom:
Unpacking Histories, Unlearning Privilege
CANDACE R. KUBY

Inspiring Dialogue:
Talking to Learn in the English Classroom
MARY M. JUZWIK, CARLIN BORSHEIM-BLACK,
SAMANTHA CAUGHLAN, & ANNE HEINTZ

Reading the Visual:
An Introduction to Teaching Multimodal Literacy
FRANK SERAFINI

Race, Community, and Urban Schools:
Partnering with African American Families
STUART GREENE

ReWRITING the Basics:
Literacy Learning in Children's Cultures
ANNE HAAS DYSON

Writing Instruction That Works:
Proven Methods for Middle and High School Classrooms
ARTHUR N. APPLEBEE & JUDITH A. LANGER, WITH KRISTEN CAMPBELL
WILCOX, MARC NACHOWITZ, MICHAEL P. MASTROIANNI, &
CHRISTINE DAWSON

Literacy Playshop: New Literacies, Popular Media, and
Play in the Early Childhood Classroom
KAREN E. WOHLWEND

continued

For volumes in the NCRLL Collection (edited by JoBeth Allen and Donna E. Alvermann) and the Practitioners Bookshelf Series
(edited by Celia Genishi and Donna E. Alvermann), as well as other titles in this series, please visit www.tcpress.com.

Language and Literacy Series, *continued*

Critical Media Pedagogy:
Teaching for Achievement in City Schools
ERNEST MORRELL, RUDY DUEÑAS, VERONICA GARCIA,
& JORGE LOPEZ

A Search Past Silence: The Literacy of Young Black Men
DAVID E. KIRKLAND

The ELL Writer:
Moving Beyond Basics in the Secondary Classroom
CHRISTINA ORTMEIER-HOOPER

Reading in a Participatory Culture:
Remixing *Moby-Dick* in the English Classroom
HENRY JENKINS & WYN KELLEY, WITH KATIE CLINTON, JENNA
MCWILLIAMS, RICARDO PITTS-WILEY, & ERIN REILLY, EDS.

Summer Reading:
Closing the Rich/Poor Achievement Gap
RICHARD L. ALLINGTON & ANNE MCGILL-FRANZEN, EDS.

Real World Writing for Secondary Students:
Teaching the College Admission Essay and
Other Gate-Openers for Higher Education
JESSICA SINGER EARLY & MEREDITH DECOSTA

Teaching Vocabulary to English Language Learners
MICHAEL F. GRAVES, DIANE AUGUST, &
JEANETTE MANCILLA-MARTINEZ

Literacy for a Better World:
LAURA SCHNEIDER VANDERPLOEG

Socially Responsible Literacy
PAULA M. SELVESTER & DEBORAH G. SUMMERS

Learning from Culturally and Linguistically Diverse
Classrooms: Using Inquiry to Inform Practice
JOAN C. FINGON & SHARON H. ULANOFF, EDS.

Bridging Literacy and Equity
ALTHIER M. LAZAR ET AL.

"Trust Me! I Can Read"
SALLY LAMPING & DEAN WOODRING BLASE

Reading Girls
HADAR DUBROWSKY MA'AYAN

Reading Time
CATHERINE COMPTON-LILLY

A Call to Creativity
LUKE REYNOLDS

Literacy and Justice Through Photography
WENDY EWALD, KATHARINE HYDE, & LISA LORD

The Successful High School Writing Center
DAWN FELS & JENNIFER WELLS, EDS.

Interrupting Hate
MOLLIE V. BLACKBURN

Playing Their Way into Literacies
KAREN E. WOHLWEND

Teaching Literacy for Love and Wisdom
JEFFREY D. WILHELM & BRUCE NOVAK

Overtested
JESSICA ZACHER PANDYA

Restructuring Schools for Linguistic Diversity,
Second Edition
OFELIA B. MIRAMONTES, ADEL NADEAU, & NANCY L. COMMINS

Words Were All We Had
MARÍA DE LA LUZ REYES, ED.

Urban Literacies
VALERIE KINLOCH, ED.

Bedtime Stories and Book Reports
CATHERINE COMPTON-LILLY & STUART GREENE, EDS.

Envisioning Knowledge
JUDITH A. LANGER

Envisioning Literature, Second Edition
JUDITH A. LANGER

Writing Assessment and the Revolution in Digital Texts
and Technologies
MICHAEL R. NEAL

Artifactual Literacies
KATE PAHL & JENNIFER ROWSELL

Educating Emergent Bilinguals
OFELIA GARCÍA & JO ANNE KLEIFGEN

(Re)Imagining Content-Area Literacy Instruction
RONI JO DRAPER, ED.

Change Is Gonna Come
PATRICIA A. EDWARDS ET AL.

When Commas Meet Kryptonite
MICHAEL BITZ

Literacy Tools in the Classroom
RICHARD BEACH ET AL.

Harlem on Our Minds
VALERIE KINLOCH

Teaching the New Writing
ANNE HERRINGTON, KEVIN HODGSON, & CHARLES MORAN, EDS.

Children, Language, and Literacy
CELIA GENISHI & ANNE HAAS DYSON

Children's Language
JUDITH WELLS LINDFORS

Children's Literature and Learning
BARBARA A. LEHMAN

Storytime
LAWRENCE R. SIPE

Effective Instruction for Struggling Readers, K–6
BARBARA M. TAYLOR & JAMES E. YSSELDYKE, EDS.

The Effective Literacy Coach
ADRIAN RODGERS & EMILY M. RODGERS

Writing in Rhythm
MAISHA T. FISHER

Reading the Media
RENEE HOBBS

teachingmedia*literacy*.com
RICHARD BEACH

What Was It Like?
LINDA J. RICE

Research on Composition
PETER SMAGORINSKY, ED.

New Literacies in Action
WILLIAM KIST

Every Young Child A Reader

Using Marie Clay's Key Concepts for Classroom Instruction

Sharan A. Gibson
Barbara Moss

Foreword by Gay Su Pinnell

TEACHERS COLLEGE PRESS

TEACHERS COLLEGE | COLUMBIA UNIVERSITY

NEW YORK AND LONDON

Published by Teachers College Press, 1234 Amsterdam Avenue, New York, NY 10027

Copyright © 2016 by Teachers College, Columbia University

Figure 5.3 was reprinted with permission from Wiley from *The Reading Teacher* ©2008 International Reading Association.

Library of Congress Cataloging-in-Publication Data is available at loc.gov

ISBN 978-0-8077-5810-6 (paper)
ISBN 978-0-8077-5811-3 (hardcover)
ISBN 978-0-8077-7517-2 (ebook)

Printed on acid-free paper
Manufactured in the United States of America

23 22 21 20 19 18 17 16   8 7 6 5 4 3 2 1

This book is dedicated to Marie M. Clay, with gratitude for her many years of expertise, advocacy, and insight regarding teaching and children's literacy learning. Her work and her dedication to meeting the needs of all children have inspired us all. We are grateful, as well, to the many wonderful teachers and colleagues who have helped us to understand what can be achieved through their unending commitment to quality education for all children.

Contents

Foreword   Gay Su Pinnell   ix

Introduction   1

    Elian and Karen: The Crucial Role of Strategic Activity   4

    Four Essential Principles   6

    Features of the Book   11

1. **Differentiated Classroom Instruction**   14

    Why Is Differentiated Classroom Instruction Essential?   15

    Implementing Differentiated Classroom Instruction   18

    Systematic Observation of Children's Literacy Behaviors   26

    Summary   30

2. **Teaching Foundational Skills**   32

    Integrated Opportunities to Learn Foundational Skills   33

    Learning Concepts About Print   36

    Learning Letters   38

    Summary   44

3. **The Role of Meaning and Comprehension in Learning: Narrative Text**   46

    Integrated Decoding and Comprehension Instruction   47

    Reading Narrative Text for Enjoyment and Understanding   49

    Teaching for Meaning and Comprehension   50

    Summary   59

4. **Building Knowledge with Informational Text**   61

    Incorporating Informational Texts in the Classroom   61

    Building Knowledge and Enlarging Experience   62

    Gaining Knowledge Through Units of Study   66

    Summary   77

5. **Learning to Write Informational Text**   79

    Writing as Active Problem Solving   79

    Constructing Ideas into Written Language   85

    Student Strengths and the Challenges of Informational Text   89

    Dedicated Time for Writing   92

    Summary   94

6. **A Steep Gradient into More Complex Literacy Tasks**   96

    Engineering a Step Up in Complex Learning   97

    Achieving Rigor in K–2 Classroom Literacy Instruction   98

    Teaching for Successful Reading of Increasingly Complex Text   106

    Summary   111

Epilogue: Leadership in Classroom-Based Instructional Change   113

    Building a Comprehensive Literary Program One Shift at a Time   113

    Collaborative Extended Learning Through Classroom Teaching   119

Suggested Readings   123

References   127

Index   137

About the Authors   150

Foreword

Sharan Gibson and Barbara Moss take a close look at reading and learning to read with the goal of increasing teachers' instructional expertise. Some powerful guiding principles are evident in this work. First, these authors see literacy as a highly complex process. And, they claim, effective literacy teachers are guided in their work by their deep (and constantly increasing) knowledge of literacy processing. The idea that teachers make their decisions based on their own tentatively held theories of learning rather than on scripts that are handed to them has an important implication: Instruction grows from what teachers believe to be true about learning. They need the ability to engage in expert observation of literacy behavior, an understanding of the nature of literacy learning in all its aspects, and a repertoire of ways to interact with readers effectively to support learning. Acquiring such a level of expertise takes years of experience and study; the information in this volume will provide valuable support.

The authors ground this publication in the work of Marie Clay, whose award-winning research led to the development of a rich theory of literacy processing as well as a body of literature that applies to teaching literacy in the early years. Clay's work has had profound effects on the world of education. In particular, she is the creator of the Reading Recovery early intervention, which has had documented startlingly positive results in helping children who initially have difficulty learning to read and write. Her procedures, used worldwide, have enabled well over a million young struggling readers to make accelerated progress and catch up to their grade level peers.

Although they recognize the quality of Reading Recovery, Gibson and Moss do not seek to adapt the one-to-one intervention to classroom work. Instead, they turn to Clay's theoretical work in their quest to inform and empower classroom teachers. The authors provide a cogent description of the cognitive processing involved as young children take on literacy and then extend the description with examples. They present a number of compelling ideas, including four essential principles that can guide teachers in the development of a personal theory. A reader who thinks deeply about these ideas and applies them to observations of reading and writing behavior can greatly extend his or her own theoretical foundation for making effective teaching decisions. Especially interesting is their description of a complex view of literacy processing, which I consider to be Clay's greatest contribution to our understanding of how children learn to read. Once we as teachers accept a complex view, then we must consider instruction that recognizes that complexity.

Also of great interest in this volume is the authors' recognition of the role of text complexity in children's learning to read. They describe Clay's concept of rapid change as learners encounter texts of increasing complexity. Text is a key factor in literacy learning. The challenges in each text offer the opportunity to expand the literacy processing system, and the teacher's facilitative language provides the necessary support. Underlying this philosophy of teaching is the profound idea that, while we teach children in large and small groups in the classroom, they learn as individuals. The idea of looking at individual learners permeates the pages of this book, which is unusual in a volume about classroom teaching.

These writers challenge us to implement differentiated teaching in classrooms to meet the instructional needs of individuals, and they have provided a rich source of information to help us do it.

—Gay Su Pinnell
professor emeritus, School of Teaching and Learning,
The Ohio State University

Introduction

This book challenges K–2 teachers, reading specialists, and literacy coaches to revise and expand their instructional expertise in response to (1) the multifaceted nature of children's literacy learning, (2) expert observation as children work on reading and writing tasks, and (3) the characteristics of powerful instructional interaction with children. Teachers with an "encompassing commitment to thoughtful practice" and increasingly deep knowledge of literacy processes will bolster all students' literacy skills (May, Sirinides, Gray, & Goldsworthy, 2016, p. 91). Such teachers are also uniquely situated to best support school-wide instruction through collaborative relationships with grade level and intervention teachers for improved schoolwide achievement levels. Without this expertise, classroom teachers are likely to instruct from narrow definitions of children's literacy learning, expecting children to bridge the gaps between demands to simply memorize letters and words or to keep up with a predetermined instructional sequence, and the complex behaviors needed to read and write text (Clay, 2001). It follows that instruction founded in a comprehensive understanding of literacy development is essential for effective teaching of today's diverse students, including children from varying achievement levels and socioeconomic, cultural, and linguistic backgrounds, and in response to each child's personal learning history and interests.

Many children will continue to fail, struggle, or experience gaps and confusions about literacy in the absence of the differentiated teaching that ensures they develop the foundational skills and strategic activity (in-the-head, problem-solving behaviors; Clay, 2005b) needed for reading and writing. We have written this book with these risks in mind, constructing a bridge from Marie Clay's research-based understandings of children's literacy development to effective instructional contexts, learning opportunities, and teacher–student interaction. Accordingly, we have presented examples in each chapter illustrating Clay's theories of literacy processing, and describing how teachers should conceptualize and build literacy instruction within their own classrooms in light of Clay's theories of literacy development. Our readers can learn, for example, why an accuracy score alone is not sufficient for decisions about easy, instructional, or frustration-level reading texts—or why and how to improve the quantity and quality of their prompting in support of children's strategic activity during small-group instruction and brief, individual coaching.

Clay is most well known for her development of the Reading Recovery® early intervention (Clay, 1979, 1993, 2005a, 2005b). Reading Recovery has an impressive and proven track record of extraordinary results with failing 1st-grade readers (D'Agostino & Murphy, 2004; International Data Evaluation Center, 2014–2015; May, Sirinides, Gray, & Goldsworthy, 2016; Schwartz, 2005a; Sparks, 2016; U.S. Department of Education, 2013). Any child, then, who is one of the lowest-achieving readers in her 1st-grade classroom should have access to Reading Recovery instruction in order to catch up quickly to grade level or higher reading ability. Most children, however, respond positively to excellent classroom instruction and do not need Reading Recovery intervention (Clay, 2005a). Additionally, Reading Recovery instruction is based explicitly on the results of ongoing program evaluation with 1st-grade, failing readers only, and cannot determine how a classroom literacy program for diverse learners should be constructed (Clay, 2005a). This book, then, does not describe an adaptation of Reading Recovery instruction to the classroom context. We have not recommended, for example, that classroom teachers should somehow teach a series of one-on-one lessons with individual children, or that small-group reading instruction should simply copy the procedural steps used in Reading Recovery lessons. Instead, this book explains Clay's theories of literacy development, coupled with effective classroom teaching practices that reflect these understandings.

Clay's development of Reading Recovery was founded on her research and construction of a literacy processing theory and teaching based on systematic observation (see Figure I.1).

Throughout her career, Clay contrasted and developed detailed understanding of the import of changes over time in the reading behaviors of children at varying achievement levels. She presented detailed accounts of children's learning as the foundation for understanding effective literacy instruction, and articulated a strong commitment to instruction that meets the needs of individual learners:

> As a consequence of thinking about teaching a class we reason as if it were the class that learns; but only individuals learn . . . the average learner, the curriculum, the stages of development, the sequences of learning, and the poor or slow learner—these are teaching concepts that get in the way of individuals having appropriate opportunities for learning. (Clay, 2014, p. 238)

Figure I.1. Clay's Research and Theory Development

Clay's Research	Clay's Research Questions
• *Teaching of Reading to Special Class Children* (Irwin, 1948) • *Emergent Reading Behavior* (Clay, 1966, 1982) • Longitudinal study of four language groups (e.g., Clay, 1971) • Reading Recovery field trials and replication studies	• "Can we see the process of reading going astray close to the onset of instruction?" (Clay, 1966) • "What is possible when we change the design and delivery of traditional education for the children that teachers find hard to teach?" (Clay, 1993)

Clay's Theory Building

Challenged existing assumptions regarding readiness and assumed limits to what children can be expected to learn.

Developed reliable assessment tools for fine-grained analysis of changes over time in children's literacy learning.

Described the change over time in reading behaviors of children at low, low middle, high middle, and high levels of progress.

Described children's active use of strategic activity, leading to expanded foundational skills and effective reading and writing.

Developed and refined a complex literacy processing theory.

Developed theories of effective instructional interaction with young literacy learners.

Sources: Ballantyne, 2009; Gaffney & Askew, 1999.

Instruction is most effective when delivered to small, flexible groups of children working on just-challenging-enough texts, and as children learn to use strategic activity for reading and writing. Children must learn, for instance, how to simultaneously extract and construct meaning from increasingly sophisticated texts by developing a complex set of skills and strategies (e.g., Pearson, Valencia, & Wixson, 2014; RAND Reading Study Group, 2002). We have written this book with these principles in mind, illustrating how such instruction can be best understood and constructed in K–2 classrooms. The instructional procedures we have illustrated maximize the effects of instruction for diverse learners; instruction targets the specific learning needs of individual children within whole- and small-group instruction and is based on systematic observation of children's current strengths and roadblocks. Consequently, children do not simply receive instruction based on any one approach or program alone (such as may occur in response to a suspected disability). Nor is it assumed that all children will enter school with similar understandings (or even interest) in literacy activities. Instead, children of diverse backgrounds and interests participate in robust classroom instruction with learning opportunities matched to their own, immediate needs.

In the sections below, we present an overview of key aspects of Clay's theories. We begin this discussion with a description of two very different 1st-grade children's reading behaviors. These are described in order to illustrate the importance of children's development of strategic activity, as well as the ways that classroom teachers can respond to children's differing progress. We also explain four crucial aspects of Clay's theories in preparation for material described in the book's chapters: an overview of Clay's literacy processing theory, the reciprocal relationship between learning to read and learning to write, the essential role of continuous text in literacy learning, and how to achieve success via a steep gradient of difficulty.

ELIAN AND KAREN:
THE CRUCIAL ROLE OF STRATEGIC ACTIVITY

A few months into his 1st-grade year, Elian controlled directional behaviors with ease, knew most letter names and sounds, and could locate and identify a small set of high-frequency words within text. Elian also demonstrated an increasingly sophisticated use of early strategic activities. He generally did notice, for example, when one of his attempts to identify a word in text did not look like the word in print and/or make sense. He would then reread from the beginning of the sentence or page to pick up more information, and attempt to identify an alternate word with a better match to print, language, and meaning. Although he was still reading at an early text difficulty level, Elian was learning more about strategic activity each time he read text; his use of concepts about print, letter sounds, and words was becoming more comprehensive and sophisticated as he developed strong strategic behaviors.

Karen, however, was not able to use her knowledge of letters and words as she attempted to read simple, emergent-level texts. As did Elian, Karen understood directional behavior for reading and writing, and could identify most letter names and sounds as well as a few high-frequency words. Karen had not yet learned, though, how to use her knowledge of letters and words to read text. She did not locate or identify in text the words she knew in isolation. In contrast to Elian's active use of strategic activity, Karen did not self-monitor to determine whether her attempt for a word fit the available phonetic, language, and/or message-getting information, and thus did not reread or search for more information. Instead, Karen often simply tried to memorize the books she was asked to read in school; she did not yet know how to look for and use known letters and words in print or to monitor what she thought a text might say against information in print. Consequently, Karen was not yet learning about strategic activity and lacked the reading behaviors needed for good progress.

Both Elian and Karen were able to identify letter sounds and words in isolation (outside of the context of text reading and writing). The key difference between these two children's reading behavior resided in their use, or nonuse, of strategic activity while reading continuous text. Clay (2001, 2005b) defined strategic activity as central to children's learning; to make strong progress, children must learn how to problem-solve effectively while reading and writing continuous text by monitoring, searching for information, and confirming word identification, language, and messages. Elian, then, was likely to continue learning how to read at a strong rate of progress; his searching for information to monitor, self-correct, and/or confirm was generative for ongoing learning. Based on observations of Elian's current reading behaviors, it is likely that his teacher would choose somewhat more complex text for his reading lessons. These texts would allow Elian to extend his current learning to new challenges, including work in longer texts with more complex sentence structures, words with suffixes or two syllables, and new information or multiple events in narratives.

Although Karen faced significant roadblocks to her literacy learning, her difficulties were not evidence of a reading disability. Instead, the classroom instruction she needed would refocus urgently on differentiated instruction to achieve fast shifts in how she understood reading tasks. Her teacher might, for example, provide additional small-group reading instruction for Karen and prompt her to monitor with her known words in print. After Karen read a sentence correctly, her teacher could write a known high-frequency word on a small whiteboard, ask Karen to say it slowly while running her finger under the word, and then check to confirm that her reading of the word in text was correct: "Does it look like the word *see*?" When reading books where high-frequency words occur in the same position within each sentence ("I see the cat. I see the dog. I see the bird too."), Karen would be likely to simply memorize without monitoring. Instead, her teacher would need to choose books that contain Karen's known words in varying positions: "I can *see* the cat. I *see* it too!" It is likely that other children in Karen's classroom and reading group would benefit from this type of instruction as well.

Across these two children, then, teaching decisions should be based on careful observation of reading behaviors, resulting in targeted and differentiated instruction. Our examples in the following chapters focus on how teachers implement flexible instructional contexts, use only those instructional activities that actually result in children's quick progress, and expand the quantity and quality of their interaction with students. The following sections, then, explain four essential aspects of Clay's theories of children's literacy learning in light of Elian and Karen's reading behaviors.

FOUR ESSENTIAL PRINCIPLES

Clay constructed her theories of literacy processing using direct observation and analysis of young children's transitions from primitive to more sophisticated literacy processing systems (Clay, 1966, 1982, 1975). This groundbreaking research (including detailed observation of patterns of behavior as young children learned how to read and write) characterized literacy growth as control over a set of problem-solving activities used to access multiple, integrated sources of information (Doyle, 2013). Problem solving occurs when children encounter a new task or difficulty when reading or writing, and then apply useful strategic activity for a solution. A child might notice, for example, that a sentence as read did not make sense—thus causing the child to reread to identify new, additional information and correct the error. As described above, Elian engaged in this type of strategic activity by monitoring and rereading. As he did so, he extended his understanding of multiple sources of information: concepts about print, letters and words, language, and message getting.

Clay's literacy processing theory was not a guess or hunch about learning. Instead, a scientific theory is a carefully formulated conceptual framework (based on valid empirical and/or observational evidence) that explains why and how a phenomenon (such as children's literacy learning) occurs in particular ways. Clay constructed and revised her theories over time using an extensive research base created through her systematic, longitudinal observation of young children's literacy learning (Doyle, 2013). She also integrated her theories with those of a wide range of other researchers and experts. The sections below provide brief explication of four essential principles central to Clay's theories and to our chapters' instructional recommendations. These principles, forming Clay's integrated and transformative theory of literacy processing, build a strong, lasting foundation for understanding literacy teaching and development.

A Complex View of Literacy Processing

While Elian was able to use strategic activity to pull in information about print, language, and meaning, he also used simple letter-to-sound correspondence and a small but increasingly sophisticated knowledge of high-frequency words while reading. Consequently, his knowledge of sources of information still needed to become more sophisticated and detailed over time. Examples might include (1) self-correction behavior that progresses from use of gross discrepancies between words to more discrete differences signaled by letter clusters or phonograms, or (2) a move from laborious correction using multiple attempts and rereading of a whole sentence or page to more efficient self-correction right at the point of error (Clay, 2001).

Clay (2001) found that literacy processing is constructed as readers engage in strategic decisionmaking while reading and writing text. Emergent readers with only a few known letters and words develop an increased receptiveness for visual information. These children pull new kinds of information from print together with language and meaning (Clay, 2001; Doyle, 2013). Gradually, children learn how to manage the full complexity of information sources. Clay found that the "rich intermingling of language learning" (1975, p. 19) accounted for children's construction of early literacy systems: "the reader making good progress constructs a literacy processing system that involves all language knowledge sources, including story structure, language structure, word and word structure, letters, and the features and sounds of letters" (Doyle, 2013, p. 644). Clay (2001) referred to this as a complex model of interacting competencies.

Clay's complex theories can perhaps be best understood in contrast to a simple view of reading. The simple theory proposed that reading comprehension (RC) is a consequence of decoding (D) and listening comprehension (LC) only: RC = D + LC (Gough & Tunmer, 1986). The simple view of reading, however, is an incomplete and misleading model (Concannon-Gibney & Murphy, 2010; Johnson, Jenkins, & Jewell, 2005; Joshi & Aaron, 2000; Kirby & Savage, 2008; Tiu, Thompson, & Lewis, 2003), and does not adequately describe what beginning readers and writers must learn. Clay's research (2001, 2005a, 2005b) demonstrated that reading development is much more complex than decoding and listening comprehension alone. Clay (2001) found that successful readers and writers learn how to attend to multiple aspects of literacy tasks. For emergent readers, these aspects typically include concepts about print (left to right and top to bottom directionality, and one-to-one matching), knowledge of a few letters and words, and the ability to tell a story from print and pictures. As children gain successful experience, they begin to monitor and self-correct by noticing gross discrepancies between a word or idea expected and that found in print. It may not be feasible, for example, for an emergent reader to correctly identify the word *saw:* "Little Kitty saw the bird!" Instead, an emergent-level reader may focus attention on the initial letter of *saw* and construct an understandable sentence using a more familiar word form: "Little Kitty sees the bird." Past tense verbs are generally a later accomplishment in children's language development, and emergent readers may not yet know how to scan all letters and letter sounds within a word. This may be especially true for a word such as *saw*, which also has the difficult-to-learn phonogram *aw*.

Young readers learn how to work their way across print, word by word and event by event, using the text itself (i.e., spaces between words, letters, phonetic information, parts of words, known words, and phrases), oral language, syntax, and meaning as guide (Clay, 2001). As they progress, children begin to take ownership over their own solving of new words and to integrate information from different knowledge sources. They process texts faster and more accurately, linking what is seen in text with what is heard and expected based on phonemic awareness, semantic, and syntactic information. Children, then, learn how to give momentary, simultaneous attention to possible meanings of a text, to language, and to sentence structures (that is, rules about the order of ideas and words), along with knowledge of letters, sounds, and words (Clay, 2001).

Reciprocal Relationship Between Reading and Writing

Learning to read and learning to write are reciprocal and interrelated processes; learning in one area supports and extends learning in the other (Clay, 2001, 2014). Children develop rich networks of knowledge as they engage in text reading and writing, using multiple sources of information in interrelated ways (Clay, 2001). The reciprocal nature of reading and writing is, then, a rich foundation of common sources of information about how text works for young literacy learners.

Effective classroom instruction should utilize this reciprocal connection between reading and writing to support children's fast progress. Writing requires children's slow analysis as they construct new and challenging words from individual phonemes or by hearing larger parts of words such as onset and rime (r-an), inflected endings (help-ed), or syllables (Clay, 2001, 2014). Primary-grade teachers, for example, help children hear phonemes within words; students learn how to articulate the sounds within a word in order to make spelling decisions while writing. This learning also helps children learn to decode by monitoring how a challenging word sounds against the letters and letter clusters seen in the word while reading (Clay, 2005b). A teacher might usefully demonstrate how to hear sounds within a word in order to develop Karen's understanding for how a word might look in print: "If I say the word *house* slowly, I can see if it looks right. *h-ou-s*. Yes, I think it's right." These activities help children become sensitized to word analysis at increasingly sophisticated levels, thus supporting improved word identification during reading.

The Common Core State Standards (CCSS; National Governors Association Center for Best Practice & Council of Chief State School Officers [NGACBP & CCSSO], 2010) also recognize the interrelated nature of reading and writing:

> Each year in their writing, students should demonstrate increasing sophistication in all aspects of language use, from vocabulary and syntax to the development and organization of ideas, and they should address increasingly demanding context and sources. (California Department of Education [CDE], 2011, p. 21)

K–2 students are also expected to participate in shared, collaborative research in support of writing projects, exploring a number of different books and multimedia sources on a given topic. Similarly, the California ELA/ELD framework (CDE, 2014) conceptualizes literacy instruction within five key themes: meaning making, language development, effective expression, content knowledge, and foundational skills.

Essential Role of Continuous Text

Frequent, guided, and independent opportunities to read interesting and challenging texts are essential for literacy learning. Children begin to read with only a few known "signposts" (known letters and/or words) in print (Clay, 1991a). Once children enter school, there should not be any long, initial period focused exclusively on letters, letter sounds, and words without guided opportunities to read and write even very simple, continuous text. Beginning in kindergarten, then, children need regular opportunities to read emergent-level texts with teacher guidance. Kindergarten teachers can demonstrate the reading of simple, patterned texts for those children who are not already immersed in their own reading: "When I read this page, I see the picture and I know the first word, *I*. I'll point to each word. *I have a toy*." Such demonstrations, combined with opportunities to read and reread familiar emergent texts each day, are crucial for effective first teaching; text reading and text writing provide the context within which children put their expanding knowledge of letters, phonemic awareness, and words into practice, thus solidifying this knowledge and making it easier to learn.

Children's engagement in text reading also provides opportunities to learn how to comprehend. Children should learn how to focus attention on meaning and comprehension while they are still learning decoding skills. In fact, reading comprehension is no longer just one of five priorities (i.e., phonemic awareness, phonics, fluency, vocabulary, and comprehension) emphasized by the National Reading Panel (National Institute of Child Health and Human Development, 2000; Williams, 2013). Instead, high-level meaning-making is emphasized within standards and instructional reform efforts as the overall goal of all reading and writing. This emphasis on comprehension is entirely consistent with Clay's comprehensive and complex viewpoint on successful literacy learning. Clay (1991a) defined comprehension as the primary overall purpose of reading: "In fact I regard meaning as the 'given' in all reading—the source of anticipation, the guide to being on track, and the outcome and reward of the effort" (pp. 1–2). Gaining meaning from text can be taught through careful and detailed orientation of children to each new reading book or story, extended and detailed conversations about these texts with teacher and peers, explanation of comprehension strategies, and children's consistent use of meaning as a source of information.

Achieving Success on a Steep Gradient of Difficulty

Children's successful progress with increasing text complexity and across a variety of types of texts is a key feature of both Clay's theories and language arts standards. Students must learn how to discern authors' (and their own) ideas (and connections between ideas) as well as textual evidence in support of reasoning (NGACBP & CCSSO, 2010). Clay (2001, 2005b) described the need for a fast pace of change in children's learning. When teaching small-group reading lessons, for example, successful classroom teachers move children to more complex, varying texts as fast as is possible without causing frustration. Each reading lesson should stretch and expand children's text processing abilities:

> If the child moves forward slowly . . . the end result is not as satisfactory as speedy progress through the book levels. It is as if the brain cells need to be involved tomorrow in what they explored today to consolidate some permanent change in their structure. (Clay, 2005b, p. 151)

The types of challenges presented to students and the rate of change in children's strategic activity, then, matter. When children are challenged appropriately by texts and literacy tasks, this causes them to extend their use of a repertoire of strategic activities and thus to permanently increase the accuracy and speed of their literacy processing (Clay, 2001). And, when teachers implement differentiated instruction, they use only those instructional activities and texts that result in good progress with their own particular children. Teachers are able to take individual differences into account, such as children's diverse needs in foundational skills, language development, and knowledge building. They can ensure, then, that all children encounter "do-able" challenges in the books read for instructional purposes—challenges that children can solve successfully with use of strategic activity and teacher or peer assistance, as needed. These instructional characteristics ensure that all children have access to a rigorous literacy program.

FEATURES OF THE BOOK

Both national and state standards are calling for a wide-ranging and rigorous 21st-century academic preparation achieved through children's engagement in deeper thinking and extensive reading and writing. Standards do not, however, explain *how* to achieve these goals. Nor should standards mandate teachers' use of any particular program or style of instruction. Instead, educators must understand successful practices in primary-grade instruction and match these to the immediate needs of their own particular students. Classroom teachers need a commitment to instructional dexterity. They learn how to seek maximum learning for children in each lesson, and to use systematic observation to implement effective in-the-moment instructional language and decisions with personal connections and precision (May, Sirinides, Gray, & Goldsworthy, 2016).

This book provides specific suggestions and instructional examples for K–2 teachers as they help children meet new and rigorous expectations in all facets of literacy learning. Within each chapter, we demonstrate how primary-grade teachers can apply a comprehensive and complex understanding of children's literacy development directly to classroom instruction. As university-level teacher educators and classroom literacy coaches, we make recommendations that are enhanced by our own expertise built and confirmed through many years as successful teachers, collaboration with a wonderful group of outstanding classroom teachers, and extensive clinical expertise with young readers and writers.

Chapter 1 demonstrates how classroom teachers can implement practical instructional contexts for whole-class and small-group instruction that allow for teaching to the needs of individual children. It is entirely possible to engage a classroom of children in exciting and useful literacy activities while teaching within small groups. This chapter explains how teachers can do so with a variety of grouping options, powerful instructional interaction with students, and activities designed so that all children are working productively.

Chapter 2 illustrates how teaching for foundational skills can be structured based on Clay's understandings of complex literacy learning. This teaching focuses on brief skill-oriented lessons and for immediate application to reading and writing activities. We also give attention in this chapter to children's multidimensional learning for concepts about print, letters, and word-identification strategies.

In Chapter 3, we discuss the central role of meaning and comprehension for children's literacy development. The chapter describes effective teaching designed to orient children to the information and details of narrative text. The chapter also describes ways to best engage in high-level conversation about text with students, including approaches for effective questioning. We also describe rich and authentic activities that can improve children's comprehension, fluency, and vocabulary knowledge.

Chapter 4 continues this emphasis on comprehension with a focus on informational text. The chapter describes how children's successful reading of informational text builds knowledge, and includes our specific suggestions for the instructional support needed for children's learning in thematic units of study and collaborative research projects.

In Chapter 5 we turn to writing development and instruction, providing information on effective prewriting instruction (including the role of student choice, verbal and visual note-taking, and language rehearsal). The chapter contrasts effective with ineffective classroom writing instruction and extends this conversation to description of ways to improve children's writing strategies by providing instruction and guidance while children write.

In Chapter 6, we explain why a fast pace of learning is needed. This chapter addresses text complexity for K–2 children's reading instruction with a discussion illustrating the characteristics of appropriate challenge for best progress. We also carefully define the characteristics and purposes of complex, frustration, instructional, familiar, and easy text levels.

The epilogue brings the chapters' topics together by describing teacher- and classroom-based literacy leadership. The chapter describes structures needed as teachers collaborate on development of a vigorous and wide-ranging literacy curriculum, as well as specific suggestions for how novice to expert teachers might begin to implement Clay's theories and our instructional recommendations within classroom instruction.

Each chapter in the book is organized around a common set of components. We have chosen these components to maximize readers' active engagement in a robust and challenging set of ideas:

- Focus questions to enhance readers' anticipation of the topics we raise within the chapter
- Illustrative example(s) of teachers and children at work on literacy learning, including instruction for children from diverse personal learning histories and linguistic or cultural backgrounds
- Explanation of teaching that builds on the foundation of Clay's literacy processing theories for K–2 classroom literacy instruction
- Recommendations for readers' further study, including one resource that directly describes specific aspects of Clay's theories and a second that provides additional information from related perspectives

Finally, we offer a list of suggested readings based directly on Clay's work. These resources are organized by topic, so that readers can delve into further study of the topics and principles described across the book.

CHAPTER 1

Differentiated Classroom Instruction

Differentiated instruction uses specific activities and classroom structures to best meet children's observed, immediate points of need. Instruction is most effective when teachers (1) utilize only those specific activities that cause strong, steady progress for their own, current students, and (2) revise the intensity and challenges of instruction based on accurate and comprehensive understanding of their own students' immediate needs. A differentiated approach to instruction is crucial for successful application of Clay's comprehensive and complex understandings of children's literacy development to classroom literacy instruction.

Clay (2014) called for differentiated teaching using appropriately challenging instructional support and additional "make-up" instruction to keep children's progress on track:

- lift the number of make-up opportunities
- offer more challenge
- give more thought in planning
- do what works for the learners
- give learners more time
- give learners more individual attention
- and allow more time for individual talk. (p. 217)

Teachers who implement differentiated instruction do not simply work harder or teach faster. Instead, they put a variety of instructional structures into place based explicitly on children's strengths and weaknesses and their own knowledge of literacy processes.

Teachers commonly use instructional practices that are not warranted in light of Clay's research on children's literacy development. This chapter, for example, describes why neither routine use of a predetermined instructional sequence nor "round-robin reading" should occur in K–2 classroom literacy programs. Instead, effective differentiated instruction requires that teachers learn how to notice, understand, and respond to children's current cognitive, literacy, and affective behaviors (Clay, 2001, 2014; Gibson & Ross, 2016). As described in this chapter, the shift to differentiated instruction may cause teachers to redesign their small-group reading instruction, improve their interaction with students regarding literacy strategies, or spend significantly less time teaching to the whole class in favor of varying types of small-group instruction. These shifts are essential components of effective, research-supported instructional practice for the benefit of children's own interests, strengths, and academic needs.

This chapter explains how differentiated teaching can be accomplished in primary-grade classrooms. We begin by explaining how Clay's theories underlie and provide a solid foundation for powerful, effective literacy instruction. Next, we explain how classroom instruction can be differentiated to meet children's needs with whole-group, small-group, and brief individual instruction. Finally, we describe how Clay's concept of systematic observation serves as the cornerstone of differentiated instruction. The following focus questions will be useful to consider while reading this chapter:

1. Why should teachers avoid teaching literacy primarily through whole-class lessons?
2. Why should children's membership in any reading group be viewed as temporary and changed quickly as needed?
3. In what ways is "round-robin reading" an ineffective and harmful practice?
4. Why are temporary, heterogeneous groups needed for differentiated instruction?
5. What do other students in a classroom do during small-group instruction?
6. Why are work time or center activities not organized by each child's reading group membership?
7. How can children who may have a specific reading disability be distinguished from those who are simply in need of more learning opportunities and finely tuned classroom instruction?
8. How does systematic observation help teachers craft targeted instructional responses?

WHY IS DIFFERENTIATED CLASSROOM INSTRUCTION ESSENTIAL?

Clay (2014) believed that routine use of any predetermined instructional sequence cannot best meet learners' needs:

> [E]very time teachers move on in a curriculum sequence they leave some children behind. (We like to think this is not so.) What a sequenced curriculum

ignores is the deeper and broader orchestration of "knowing about print" that is being constructed by any single learner. (p. 148)

Commercial reading programs can be a valuable resource for teachers and do generally address key instructional components such as phonemic awareness, phonics, fluency, vocabulary knowledge, and comprehension. Literacy learning varies both for each child and over time (Clay, 2001), however, and such programs cannot take into account how individual students are responding to instruction. The question is not *whether* children should learn crucial skills and strategies, but *how* instruction can best help each child to do so. Although high-quality core reading programs may provide a base for effective instruction, teachers should adapt and expand the sequence, pacing, and/or instructional approaches when students are struggling with any aspects of literacy learning (Denton, 2012). With strong knowledge of students' needs, teachers should use program resources flexibly by altering and adapting instructional techniques.

Teacher expertise is the best guarantee of children's learning. Good teaching "arises out of the understanding teachers have of their craft and never out of prescriptive programs" (Clay, 2014, p. 145). Exemplary classroom teachers construct a flexible schedule with frequent instructional interaction and appropriate challenge for students (Pressley, Allington, Wharton-MacDonald, Collins-Block, & Morrow, 2001). They also do not rely exclusively on any one instructional approach. Instead, an observant teacher will notice children's difficulties and provide targeted instructional solutions. They may, for example, identify new ways to demonstrate or prompt for children's use of strategic behaviors, or utilize varying instructional techniques with students who are not learning high-frequency words at an expected, strong pace. Effective teachers, therefore, know and use a variety of approaches to address children's needs: "The tough part is knowing when to do what, with whom—and having the flexibility in your classroom organization to do it!" (Clay, 2014, p. 223).

Teachers who implement differentiated instruction know that children's difficulties need to be addressed quickly. Without differentiated instruction, children are likely to adopt unhelpful approaches to literacy tasks as they struggle on without appropriate support. Simply waiting for children to be "ready" to learn does not work (Clay, 1991a, 2014; Johnston & Allington, 1991; Schmitt, Askew, Fountas, Lyons, & Pinnell, 2005). Clay (1991a) expressed concern about policies that exclude "unready" children from the very activities they need to learn: "It is not some ripening process which will eventually prepare the child but opportunities to learn through expert-novice interaction" (p. 68). The longer teachers wait to intervene with differentiated instruction (and powerful short-term intervention, as in Reading Recovery teaching, for those children most in need), the more difficult it is for children to catch up to their peers. Teaching that allows children who are confused about literacy learning to make some progress while still remaining below grade level, then, needs to be further refined to better meet students' needs.

Clay (1987) noted that it is not feasible to distinguish children who may be learning disabled from struggling readers who have not yet participated in sufficient learning opportunities matched to their particular needs. Although a small percentage of children who find learning to read difficult have a disability of biological origin, the numbers of children identified with a reading disability are highly inflated (Vellutino, Fletcher, Snowling, & Scanlon, 2004). In other words, many children who appear to be learning disabled are instead struggling because of instructional, and/or experiential deficits (Clay, 1987; International Literacy Association, 2016; Vellutino, Scanlon, Sipay, Small, Pratt, Chen, & Denckla, 1996; Vellutino, Scanlon, Zhang, & Schatschneider, 2008). A slow rate of progress can occur even when instruction is of good quality but is not adapted to a child's particular confusions (Clay, 2005b). Most English language learners (ELLs), for instance, are not disabled; these students need rich and targeted literacy instruction that teaches English language knowledge, content, and strategic activity. Diverse students need support based on teachers' understanding of each child's linguistic and background knowledge, interaction with topics and peers, and word use (National Council of Teachers of English, 2008). Most children's current and long-term reading difficulties can be overcome and prevented, then, with appropriately adapted instruction (Clay, 2001, 2014; Vellutino et al., 2008). Unfortunately, too many children experience reading failure and/or an inaccurate diagnosis for reading disability because classroom instruction has not been differentiated to their particular needs.

The instructional recommendations described in this chapter, then, are constructed on the following principles:

1. Acknowledge that every child learns differently, even when targeted learning outcomes are identical.
2. Do not rely solely on commercial literacy programs or routine use of particular instructional approaches. Instead, use such resources flexibly in response to children's immediate needs.
3. Develop familiarity with a wide variety of instructional activities, but use only those that are actually effective for next steps in children's learning.
4. Provide greater time and intensity of instruction for children encountering difficulty learning any aspects of literacy.

5. Do not identify a child for a reading disability until results of the child's participation in differentiated classroom instruction over a significant period can be evaluated.

IMPLEMENTING DIFFERENTIATED CLASSROOM INSTRUCTION

Differentiated instruction is implemented using multiple instructional contexts, with an explicit focus on being responsive to the needs of children. Flexible, purposeful grouping and teaching strategies, as described below, are more effective than use of any one instructional method (Block, Parris, Reed, Whitely, & Cleveland, 2009; Connor, Morrison, Fishman, Giuliani, Luck, Underwood, . . . Schatschneider, 2011; National Institute of Child Health and Human Development, 2000). Creating a classroom schedule, for example, that includes a variety of types of instructional groups results in higher student achievement (Clay, 2001; Morrow, Tracey, Woo, & Pressley, 1999; Pressley et al., 2001).

Grouping for Instruction

Differentiated classroom routines occur within whole-class and small-group instruction (with occasional individual coaching), and are integrated with children's work-time activities. Instructional time in busy primary classrooms is highly valuable and carefully constructed for maximum effectiveness. Teachers can maximize children's learning by using the following approaches:

- Teach multiple, integrated skills and strategies within each lesson.
- Carry out the most intensive teaching within flexible small groups of varying membership and for both homogeneous and heterogeneous groups of students.
- Determine whether brief teacher demonstration or more extensive student discussion and input would best teach the needed knowledge or strategies.

Limited Whole-Class Teaching. It is not in children's best interest to use classroom time primarily for whole-class lessons. The frequency of whole-class lessons should be carefully balanced in favor of small-group instruction and one-to-one interaction with children. This structure provides opportunities for diverse students to reach the same high standards—structuring classrooms for the widest possible range of successful student participation (CDE, 2011). The larger a group is, the more likely that instruction will cause inadvertent confusion for some children or be unsuccessful in expanding children's current literacy skills. Whole-class lessons are, however, an effective context for some types of instruction. Teaching a shared reading lesson, for example, establishes children's common ownership and interest in a particular text, and provides a strong foundation for language learning and comprehension. It may also be more efficient to introduce new reading or writing strategies in whole-class lessons, rather than teaching identical lessons to small groups of students.

Exemplary teachers teach with a high degree of instructional density; students practice multiple types of skills within each lesson (Pressley et al., 2001). Effective classrooms are busy with lots of ongoing, active instruction and classroom activities that address multiple goals. A teacher might, for example, teach a shared writing lesson with a focus on the use of capital letters for new sentences while still demonstrating how to consider word choices for a meaningful message. Or, a shared reading lesson might first review children's recent learning within the text *Frog and Toad Together* (Lobel, 1972) before introducing new learning:

Teacher: Yesterday, we practiced learning how the story's events help you to understand how a character feels. Why did Toad get so upset when his list blew away?

Student 1: He put everything on the list to do that day.

Student 2: He wanted to cross everything off.

Teacher: Right. Now, let's think about what each character said. Find the part in your book where Toad's list blew away. Read the next four pages to yourself to see what Toad and Frog said next. [After students read] Why didn't Toad want to run and catch the list when it blew away?

Student 3: Because he didn't put that on his list.

Teacher: Yes, why is that pretty funny?

Student 4: He didn't really need the list.

Student 3: It's kind of weird because he didn't have the list and then, then he couldn't go and find the list.

Teacher: Good! You are thinking about what the author meant when he told us what Toad said! Look at this word [pointing to *wailed*]. I am going to look for any parts of the word that I already know. Here's *ail*, like the word *tail*, and I see an –ed too. So what word is it?

Students: Wailed.

Teacher: Good work. We used parts of the word to figure it out. Wailed means that Toad howled loudly because he was upset. Here's how it might sound when Toad wailed: [reading] "Because running after my list is not one of the things that I wrote on my list of things to do. Let's read that page together."

This instructional density ensures that important topics are introduced and reinforced over time. It also creates strong opportunities for children to learn how to use and integrate a variety of skills while reading and writing.

It is important to limit both whole-class and small-group lessons to an appropriately short time frame. Some types of information are best provided with to-the-point, teacher-directed explanation. If the intent is to encourage children to say a word slowly to support spelling decisions, the teacher should simply demonstrate and explain: "If I need to spell the word *fast*, I can say the word slowly and write the sounds I hear." Clay (2005b) cautioned against too much teacher talk during instruction. When teachers keep talking beyond the information that is most essential to the learning, then children have to do more in-the-head processing. In consequence, children find it harder to understand and remember the main points of instruction (Bennet, 2015). Other types of instructional goals, however, require longer discussion and sufficient time for students to listen, think, and talk. Examples include discussion to build children's comprehension of a particular passage in a text or to decide whether an author's writing is clear and how it could be improved. It is important for this type of instruction to maximize the amount of time children can talk about stories, language, and their new learning.

Focused Small-Group Teaching. Small-group instruction is up to four times more effective than whole-class instruction (Connor, Piasta, Glasney, Schatschneider, Crowe, Underwood, . . . Morrison, 2009; Connor et al., 2011). Flexible, targeted small-group instruction, in fact, results in greater learning gains than does even high-quality whole-class instruction (Watts-Taffe, Laster, Broach, Marinak, Connor, & Walker-Dalhouse, 2013). One exemplary 1st-grade teacher, for example, described at least eight different types of reading groups that her students participated in each week: whole class, oral book reading to and with students, minilessons, parent-led fluency practice, learning centers, brief one-to-one conferences, and pair work with peers (Pressley et al., 2001). Similarly, the kindergarten literacy schedule shown in Figure 1.1 allows students to proceed smoothly through multiple types of instructional groupings during the school day, thus expanding their learning opportunities within varying environments, social situations, and peer collaboration.

Homogeneous Groups. Instruction delivered to small, homogeneous groups, as in guided reading instruction (Fountas & Pinnell, 1996), focuses intently on those reading and writing strategies most needed at the group's instructional reading level. Guided reading is a particularly effective type of small group reading instruction with a focus on careful text selection for each

Figure 1.1. Kindergarten Literacy Schedule

Time	Activity	Grouping
8:45	Children settle in to read books from table boxes independently or with peers.	Work time
9:00	Shared reading of a poem: Teacher read-aloud, choral reading, and partner reading. Teacher rereads one interesting line, asks students to visualize the action, and then share to the group.	Whole class
9:20	Students' work time begins. Teacher listens to one student read and praises for monitoring and self-correcting: "You noticed what was wrong and made it make sense. Great work!"	Individual
9:30	Small group lesson for four students to improve reading fluency.	Small group
9:40	Consultation with students on their progress at a center activity.	Small group
9:50	Two guided reading lessons.	Small group
10:40	Demonstration of a new spelling strategy for students at the writing center.	Small group
10:50	Morning recess.	

lesson using leveled texts and teaching for children's comprehension and strategic activity (see Fountas & Pinnell, 1996, 2012a, for more information). Small group reading instruction will not be effective, however, unless the teacher notices students' current growth and alters group membership quickly and appropriately. In many classrooms, children are assigned to a reading group and stay there the entire year. Clay (1991a) was certain, however, that the cumulative nature of literacy learning requires that group memberships must be reconsidered and revised regularly. Flexible group membership allows a faster pace of progress as children's new learning is built quickly upon the knowledge and strengths they have recently constructed.

Moving a child to a different reading group does not require extensive formal assessment. A teacher might, for example, simply observe children's reading behaviors carefully for signs that a child is ready for additional challenge:

- Is this child interested in a wider range of text types and topics?
- When she monitors an error during reading, is she able to problem-solve in some of the same ways as children in the higher reading group?

- Does she recognize a sufficient set of high-frequency words for more difficult text?

A teacher might pre-teach the new text to the child in an individual lesson before moving her into the new, more difficult reading group. This brief lesson would provide an initial reading of the book with immediate teacher guidance prior to the actual group lesson. In 5 minutes or so, then, the teacher will have prepared the child for a successful experience within a new group.

In reading group instruction, the teacher carefully chooses a new book at just the right level of difficulty, and introduces the text (and new and challenging strategic activity) just at students' point of need (Clay, 2005b). The teacher does not read the book to children. Instead, each child reads quietly (and as independently as possible) after the book has been appropriately introduced. The teacher "leans in" to individual students and briefly prompts to help the student at difficulty or with particular reading strategies. This independent reading is an indispensable opportunity for the teacher to hear each child reading, and for children to practice their own use of reading strategies on new and slightly challenging text.

Differentiated instruction should provide children with *needed* instruction—rather than simply an identical lesson format. It is typically best, for example, to have students at a strong ending 1st- or 2nd-grade reading level return to their own seats to do most of their actual reading. Students at this level are most likely able to decode successfully and read longer stretches of text independently. A lesson might start with the teacher's introduction of the new text and discussion about a particular reading strategy. Children's new learning and responses to the text can be incorporated into a writing task that is then discussed at the next lesson. The teacher can then attend to other needs within the classroom as students read and write at centers or their own desks. Children in the reading group will have engaged in extended reading and writing beyond the time frame of a lesson, and in collaboration with peers.

Eliminate "Round-Robin" Reading. Reading group lessons should never be structured in a "round-robin" format (or variants such as "popcorn" or "challenge" reading). In round-robin children take turns reading one section of a text aloud while others follow within the text. This type of lesson has numerous problems (e.g, Hilden & Jones, 2012; Kelly, 1995) and nonexistent benefits, and is harmful to students (McLaughlin, 2013). We know, in fact, of no experts in reading instruction who recommend round-robin reading lessons. There are several reasons why this is true (see Figure 1.2).

Figure 1.2. Harmful Effects of "Round-Robin" Reading Lessons

Problem	Consequences
Damage to children's self-confidence.	Children may become unwilling to attempt reading tasks.
Lack of opportunity for children to monitor their own errors.	Children do not learn how to self-monitor, search for more information, or self-correct, thus limiting their overall reading progress.
Children hear word-by-word, disfluent reading day after day.	Children and teacher both come to expect reading to be slow and unexpressive, causing difficulties in children's ability to comprehend and monitor for meaning.
Correct oral reading inaccurately perceived as the best indicator of reading competence.	Children's reading progress may be incorrectly labeled as strong, when they are in fact not learning how to comprehend text.
Lack of teaching for detailed comprehension of text.	Children (and teacher) habitually view reading as decoding only. This gap negatively affects children's development of problem-solving strategies as well as comprehension.

Performing an unrehearsed oral reading of a challenging text in front of peers carries a high risk of damage to children's self-esteem and self-confidence; public correction of children's oral reading by either teacher or peers is a common occurrence during round-robin reading. In addition, fluent oral reading is well paced, reasonably accurate, phrased, and expressive. The reading performance of peers, however, often includes high error and low self-correction rates, and halting, word-by-word fluency. Round-robin reading thus allows children to hear poor reading fluency in each lesson. Children's disfluent reading may become habitual with repeated practice, and in consequence will be very difficult to correct.

Oral reading alone, as emphasized in round-robin lessons, does not provide sufficient instruction or evidence of reading competence. Even if students do keep track of the correct place in text, they are not engaged in the strategic processing central to Clay's theories of reading development. That is, students do not self-monitor, search for more information, or self-correct when simply listening to another student read. These are the strategic activities that drive children's learning; denying children opportunities to monitor and correct their own reading limits their progress. In addition, reading is above all a meaning-based task: "a message-getting, problem-solving activity which increases in power and flexibility the more it is practiced" (Clay, 1991a, p. 6). Neither a stressful public performance while reading aloud nor simply following along in text best supports children's comprehension. Instead, comprehension should be taught within small group lessons through careful examination of the ideas within text, conversations with other readers about authors' meanings, and readers' monitoring and use of fix-it strategies.

Heterogeneous Groups. Classroom literacy instruction should include flexible grouping based on children's interests, strategy needs, skill, and social development, regardless of their overall reading levels. Struggling readers and writers, in particular, need opportunities to collaborate with peers at varying achievement levels. When group instruction and projects focus on authentic reading and writing tasks, each child will engage in the work at his own level. It is not necessary to assign all children in a classroom to heterogeneous groups at any point in time. Instead, children should join occasional heterogeneous group activities on a short-term basis. A group of children at varying reading levels, for example, might meet for several days for short lessons on fluent, expressive reading. Membership in this group would be determined by the teacher's identification of students who read in a slow, word-by-word fashion. In another example, a group of students who are passionately interested in the Guinness World Records (Glenday, 2015) can meet for several days to read about and illustrate the world's largest model train store. This kind of interest-based group will typically need teacher input to begin, as well as periodic checks to ensure progress to a completed project.

Heterogeneous groups do not always need to be taught directly by the classroom teacher. Pairs of students, for example, can read together to increase their amount of reading practice and improve fluency. Likewise, children who are learning English as a second language (or children who lack a strong sense of story) might meet individually or in pairs with a classroom volunteer for 10 minutes of story read-aloud and friendly discussion. This activity would provide ELLs with the extended discussion with an adult needed for their development of linguistic and text-based skills (Wright, 2016). The volunteer should be comfortable with typical storybook reading and talk that occurs in family contexts, and able to provide extended wait time for children's participation. Additionally, adult volunteers can teach the Paired Reading activity (Topping, 1987) to a few individual students for about 5 minutes each day. For this activity, the volunteer and student begin reading a slightly challenging text together. As soon as the student feels ready to do so, she signals (often with a knock on the desk or table) and then reads on alone until an error occurs. At that point, the volunteer simply reads the error word correctly (without commentary) and the student and volunteer begin reading together again from that point. The student can then signal to read alone again when ready.

What Do Other Students Do During Small-Group Instruction?

Acknowledging that children do not need to be directed step by step through all activities for learning to occur may be the most difficult challenge confronting teachers as they move into differentiated instruction. In actuality, learning is supported by teacher-directed lessons, children's collaborative talk with peers, and their sustained, active engagement in authentic reading and writing tasks.

Children's reading and writing of texts during independent classroom work time should be a normal, everyday task. This expectation creates powerful learning opportunities when integrated with topics taught within whole-class and small-group instruction. Children might, for example, read about a particular topic during shared reading lessons and then continue during work time with additional reading and writing tasks on the same topic. Children's work-time activities can be structured with a list of tasks to accomplish or as center activities. Work-time activities or centers, however, should *not* be organized by reading level or reading group membership. Rather, children should read and write independently or in collaborative, heterogeneous groups. The teacher will pull individual children out of work time or centers at any time, as needed for small-group instruction or individual coaching. Since work-time tasks emphasize extended opportunities to read and write, these can be easily completed later that same day or even on another day.

A teacher might begin by creating a set of generic centers. These are areas of the classroom set up for children's engagement in particular disciplines. A writing center, for example, would be stocked with pencils, pens, various types of paper, envelopes, crayons, and so forth. A measurement center would offer rulers, tape measures, and scales. Later, these generic centers can be adapted for particular tasks. Children might be learning, for example, how to create bar graphs and can practice at the measurement center by recording the lengths or weights of a set of objects. To add a literacy activity to their measurement work, students might write a description of the information on their graphs. Similarly, children can draw or paint a character from a favorite story at the art center and then write a list of words describing the character or an informational text explaining why and how the character has been represented within the artwork.

Clay (2014) pointed out that a belief in the constructive nature of young learners requires an essential change in instruction: "We do not have to solve the problems of teaching with diversity entirely on our own: we have the constructive learner as our strongest ally" (p. 248). Learning occurs when teachers present children with authentic and engaging tasks, and time to work collaboratively. A work-time activity that requires little engagement or practice with newly emerging skills (such as cutting out and pasting preprepared snowmen forms) is not likely to support learning. Such activities are a delightful, occasional addition to holiday-related activities. Children's learning during work time, however, needs to be at least as powerful as instruction directed by the teacher (Ford & Opitz, 2010). Math and science centers, for example, encourage students to read and/or write as a mathematician or scientist. Children at the science center might first read several books on the life cycle of spiders (at varying difficulty levels), draw a series of pictures illustrating this life cycle, and then label the most relevant parts of each picture.

Tasks with scope (Clay, 2014) support learning much more readily than do tasks that are narrowly defined. Classrooms are more successful when students engage in work-time tasks using complex thinking and elaborated communication about important and interesting issues. Students in such classrooms have higher standardized test scores, for example, with 20% higher learning gains than the national average (Newmann, Bryk, & Nagaoka, 2001). The CCSS, for example, specify that a single, rich task will teach knowledge and skill across several different standards and disciplines (NGACBP & CCSSO, 2010). Tasks with scope are rich and broad enough to allow each learner to engage successfully at her own level of competence. When children write an informational book as a collaborative, small-group activity, for example, different children will naturally perform different portions of the task. Children will also assist one another throughout the project, thus creating a rich context for learning.

SYSTEMATIC OBSERVATION OF
CHILDREN'S LITERACY BEHAVIORS

Systematic observation of children's literacy behaviors (Clay, 2013) is a crucial first step for any teacher's implementation of differentiated instruction. In this section, we describe the overall purpose and characteristics of systematic observation, as well as the use of running record and spelling observation to target instruction to children's current needs.

Clay (2014) believed that teachers can best avoid a dangerous reliance on biases or intuition when they know how to systematically observe, record, and analyze children's literacy behavior. Systematic observation serves a very different purpose than outcome-based or standardized testing. Standardized assessment provides useful information on *group* outcomes and overall achievement levels, but virtually no guidance on children's immediate instructional needs. Carefully designed observation and analysis, on the other hand, provide continuous and reliable information used to guide moment-by-moment instructional decisions.

Systematic observation does not involve simply watching children or collecting samples of their work. Instead, teachers learn how to (1) notice literacy behaviors accurately and thoroughly, and (2) weigh this information against the development needed for good progress. Teachers' systematic observation, then, results in stronger understanding about how a child engages in reading and writing tasks (Clay, 2014). For systematic observation, teachers should make a record capturing the observable problem-solving strategies and attempts a child utilizes for a short time frame while reading or writing text. Teachers can then analyze each record against the strategic activity used by high-progress readers and writers.

Useful observation requires that teachers become knowledgeable about how young children develop comprehensive literacy knowledge and effective strategy use. Clay, for example, emphasized that it is not enough to know how well children are learning letter names. Literacy processing is constructed as readers engage in integrated, strategic decisionmaking while reading and writing text. Effective teaching, then, focuses both on letter/letter sound identification, and how children are using this knowledge when reading or writing. Teachers should be particularly interested in noticing and understanding what young readers and writers actually do as they engage in problem solving when reading or writing increasingly sophisticated texts.

Running Record Assessment

Running record assessment (Clay, 2000a, 2013) uses specific notations and standard procedures to systematically observe, record, and analyze children's reading behaviors. In this section, we explain how teachers should understand the behaviors recorded in excerpts of two children's running records. These examples are used as explanation of the importance of two very different kinds of strategic activity as teachers design and implement differentiated reading instruction.

As indicated in Figure 1.3, Anna read the text (*The big brown dog ran up the stairs*) as follows: "The big, I don't know, dog ran up the steps." Howard read as follows: "The big /br/, the big brown dog ran up the steps, air, stairs, the big brown dog ran up the stairs."

Anna, then, simply skipped an unknown word without utilizing any problem-solving strategies. She made a reasonable attempt for the word *stairs*, using meaning, and beginning and ending consonants. She did not, however, use the medial mismatch between *steps* and *stairs* to correct the error. Based on this brief sample, Anna did not use the monitoring and searching for information needed to expand her understanding of how language in print works. (It would also be important to record and analyze

Figure 1.3. Sample of Two Children's Reading Behavior

Child	Reading Behavior
Anna	✔ ✔ - *IDK* ✔ ✔ ✔ ✔ *steps* The big brown dog ran up the stairs
Howard	✔ ✔ /br/ ✔ ✔ ✔ ✔ ✔ *steps/air/SC* The big brown ᴿ dog ran up the stairs ᴿ

✔ = Word read correctly	/br/ = Letter sounds articulated
- = Word skipped	ᴿ = Re-reading
IDK = Child said "I don't know"	SC = Self-correction

Anna's reading across longer portions of text to determine whether this is typical reading behavior for her.)

In contrast, Howard solved the word *brown* by utilizing the initial consonant blend, *br*, and rereading from the beginning of the sentence. Rereading is an important strategic activity for beginning readers, allowing them to revisit the print, language, and ideas of the sentence for additional information and confirmation (Clay, 2005b). Howard also read *steps* for the word *stairs*. He then noticed the mismatch between how the word *steps* should look in print and the actual word, *stairs*. This self-monitoring caused him to search for further information. He was able to confirm his self-correction for this word by using the word part *air* and rereading to pull all sources of information (phonetic, language, and meaning) together. In contrast to the first child, then, Howard was actively self-monitoring, searching for more information, and self-correcting.

Anna needed instruction in self-monitoring and self-correcting behavior during reading. This urgently needed teaching could be incorporated within a variety of grouping options, and should result in a quick change in Anna's strategic behaviors:

- Brief teacher explanation during whole-class instruction: "Oh, I just noticed that this word didn't make sense. So, I will read it again and think about a word that looks right and makes sense."
- Teacher praise for even very tentative self-monitoring behavior during small-group instruction: "I like the way you stopped. You're right. It didn't look quite right. Try that sentence again."
- Brief lessons delivered to three or four children with the same difficulty in self-monitoring and self-correction (regardless of their overall reading level).

- One to 2 minutes of individual prompting for Anna as she reads independently.

Teachers will find it useful to learn to take and analyze running records using Clay's recommended procedures (see Clay, 2000a). Standard procedures for running record assessment allow teachers to analyze children's overall fluency, accuracy, self-correction rate, use of sources of information, and strategic activity (Clay, 2013). Running records are best used in the classroom as purposeful, formative assessment (and not as formal assessment of every child's reading level). Teachers should use the information from running record analysis to make meaningful adjustments in teaching and learning. Teachers can take a running record, for example, while observing alongside a child reading at his desk, working at a center, or at the small-group table after a group activity. A typed copy of the text is *not* needed, and each assessment should take only 1 or 2 minutes.

Spelling Observation

Recording the spelling attempts of a child or two during text writing can also be used as systematic observation. A teacher might observe a child during writing and record all spelling errors for perhaps 1 or 2 minutes. This observation could occur during regular classroom writing time or perhaps at the end of a brief, small-group guided writing lesson (see Gibson, 2008). The teacher would make a record of the child's spelling errors (writing *fat* over *fast*, for example, to indicate how the word *fast* was spelled) and record brief notes on any strategies used by the child for a spelling decision. Examples of these strategies include consulting a classroom word wall, saying a word slowly to hear sounds, asking a neighbor for assistance, or applying a phonogram (such as the *ain* pattern from the known word *rain* to spell words such as *pain* or *stain*).

Children's spelling errors can be categorized as alphabetic, pattern-, or meaning-based (Bear, Invernizzi, Johnston, & Templeton, 2015). A child's spelling of *apple* as *apl*, for example, is a strong use of the phonemes heard in sequence for alphabetic spelling. In contrast, the incorrect use of a long vowel spelling pattern (perhaps spelling *paid* as *payd*) would indicate pattern-based spelling. Based on this information, the teacher might teach a series of short lessons with students who are attempting pattern spellings. In Figure 1.4, for example, students were first asked to estimate the spelling of a few challenging words with long vowel patterns.

After their attempts, the teacher led a discussion of the various patterns, emphasizing the choice of *a-consonant-e, ay,* or *ai*. Students then sorted a set of similar words into columns by long vowel pattern.

Teachers' immediate instructional decisions should be based on infor-mal data from systematic observation—without waiting for extensive child-by-child testing. The use of a spelling observation as described above, for example, is a targeted inquiry to determine how well particular children are using spelling strategies during text writing. Brief, systematic observation and analysis of spelling is ongoing and carried out in a few minutes each day as needed. The purpose is to support the teacher's creation of targeted areas of emphasis for small-group instruction and individual coaching. Similarly, it is generally not necessary to use running record assessment to test each child's reading on a series of books up a scale of text difficulty. Instead, the teacher's need for information in support of day-to-day instructional decisions should determine an occasional and flexible use of running record assessment.

SUMMARY

Differentiated instruction is contingent on teachers' knowledge of chil-dren's learning. Such instruction, however, is not easy to accomplish. Exemplary teachers implement differentiated instruction gradually, one piece at a time (Day, 2001). Any of the following actions, for example, would make an excellent starting point for teachers' reflection and fo-cused study:

- Try out one type of systematic observation to develop better under-standing of several children's current knowledge of strategic activity.
- Study several new instructional techniques with colleagues.
- Limit the frequency of whole-class lessons with a shift to heteroge-neous and homogeneous small-group lessons and occasional indi-vidual coaching.
- Change the structure of small-group reading lessons to better match children's specific instructional needs.
- Redesign work-time activities using tasks with scope that require complex thinking and collaborative talk.

FURTHER STUDY

Clay, M. M. (2000a). *Running records for classroom teachers*. Portsmouth, NH: Heinemann.

Study Clay's procedures for taking and analyzing running records of children's reading. Practice this observation technique regularly so that taking a running record becomes an easy, quick task. Pay careful attention to Clay's recommendations for scoring and analysis. Bring a running

Figure 1.4. Estimating and Discussing Long Vowel Spelling Patterns

| | Children's Attempts: Small Group of Pattern Spellers | | |
Dictated Words	ALICE	THOMAS	KERRY
shade	shaid	shade	shad
stain	stane	stane	stain
spray	spray	spray	spray
pail	pail	pale	pail
blame	blaym	blaim	blam

record or two to a meeting with colleagues, and work collaboratively to analyze and determine children's instructional needs.

Schwartz, R. M. (2005b). Decisions, decisions: Responding to primary students during guided reading. *The Reading Teacher, 58*(5), 436–443.

Read this article to study Clay's complex theory of literacy learning in light of the author's examples of supportive teacher responses during guided reading lessons. This article will help you combine observation of children's learning history and strategy use with moment-by-moment decisions for best reading progress.

CHAPTER 2

Teaching Foundational Skills

Clay (1991a, 2005b) believed that children must take on comprehensive, well-established, and highly usable knowledge of foundational skills. These include concepts about print, links between how language sounds and how it looks in print, and letter/word knowledge. Foundational skills are broadly defined by the CCSS as print concepts, phonological awareness, phonics, word recognition, and fluency. Clay (2014) cautioned, however, that learning to read and write requires complex learning beyond simply memorizing letters or words. Foundational skills are not seen as "an end in and of themselves" (CDE, 2011, p. 17). Neither learning letters in isolation, for example, nor sounding out words one letter at a time is a sufficient basis for adequate progress. Instead, children must learn how to manage the complexity across all sources of information (Clay, 1982; Doyle, 2013). Children learn how to use print in an organized fashion; they attend to features of print, words in sequence, and letters in a word from left to right while also understanding language and meanings (Clay, 2005b). Children must also be taught how to use these foundational skills when reading and writing text. Doing so supports stronger learning of foundational skills themselves as well as text reading and writing. The California English Language Arts/English Language Development framework, for example, notes that students who can decode "are best positioned to make significant strides in meaning making, language development, effective expression, and content knowledge" (Slowik & Brynelson, 2015, p. 5).

This chapter illustrates Clay's theories regarding effective teaching of foundational skills with examples of teaching through skill-oriented lessons and while children read and write text. The chapter describes the teaching of foundational skills for a small group of emergent readers in one kindergarten teacher's classroom, and clarifies the complexity of concepts about print and letter learning. It will be helpful to consider the following focus questions while reading this chapter:

1. In what ways are foundational skills more complex and challenging than might be expected?
2. How can instruction in foundational skills be differentiated to meet children's needs?

3. Why is teacher demonstration of concepts about print more effective than verbal explanation? What does this instruction look like?
4. Why should teachers avoid teaching letters solely in an alphabetic sequence from A to Z? What alternative sequence and distribution of instruction is recommended?
5. What strategies should children use to decode unknown words?

INTEGRATED OPPORTUNITIES TO LEARN FOUNDATIONAL SKILLS

Instruction in letter and word identification skills, and text reading and writing, is essential for good progress (Clay, 2001, 2005a). Children learn most effectively when provided with instruction across two dimensions:

1. Whole-class and small-group lessons, plus individual prompting and coaching
2. Lessons that address multiple goals

Exemplary teachers, then, provide frequent, brief skill-oriented lessons integrated with text-based reading and writing instruction (Pressley et al., 2001). If children are learning the sounds of consonant digraphs (i.e., *sh*, *ch*, *th*, *wh*), for example, their teacher should also prompt them to use this new knowledge when reading and writing text: "Look at the two letters at the beginning of that word. You studied these sounds in our lesson this morning. How does the word start?" In contrast, less effective teachers do not make strong connections for children between skill-based lessons and reading and writing instruction.

Andrew (a kindergarten teacher in his second year of teaching) was particularly concerned that one group of students in his classroom was not yet learning how to read effectively by midyear. This group included three ELL students who were at a "Bridging" level of English development based on the California Department of Education's English Language Development standards; they were able to understand and use English on a wide range of topics with light linguistic support for complex activities (CDE, 2012). These children were enthusiastic about stories and their own reading, and enjoyed opportunities to write. Andrew had taken a running record as each student read a text taught in recent group lessons. His analysis determined that these students used memory and pictures to construct a meaningful text but did not yet monitor with words or letter sounds while reading. As described below, Andrew decided to modify the instruction for this group both to improve students' progress and to expand his own instructional expertise.

Teaching Foundational Skills in Isolation

Children need to become both accurate and fluent in their use of foundational skills. This learning requires brief, regularly occurring, and explicit lessons targeted to students' particular needs. Teaching skills in isolation occurs outside of the context of continuous text. Children's completion of worksheets, though, does not teach foundational skills effectively. Instead, teachers need to provide clear models and explicit demonstration, ensuring that students do not have to guess what they are expected to learn. Teachers should describe the new learning very directly, and keep further teacher talk to a minimum (Clay, 2005b).

Andrew, for example, knew that his students needed to begin to monitor what they thought the text might say against the words in print. He taught a series of 5- to 10-minute lessons for this group focused on a few high-frequency words. Andrew knew that flashcard drill had not worked well for this group; word learning for his students would be easier when they learned how to notice the letters within words in sequence. Andrew taught his students how to study a new word (e.g., Clay, 2005b, pp. 176–177). He first asked them to take a good look at the target word (written in large print on a small whiteboard). Next, Andrew asked students to say the word slowly as he ran his finger under the word. He asked his students to close their eyes, say and visualize the word, and open their eyes to check. Then, he covered the word and asked students to write it with a finger in the air, write it on small whiteboards, or sequence magnetic letters correctly to form the word. Andrew repeated this procedure as needed, until his students could write the word confidently and accurately.

Fast Responses to Visual Information. Instruction in foundational skills supports children's accurate, fast, and practiced attention to visual detail in text (Clay, 2005b). A teacher might, for example, give a set of magnetic letters (including four or five each of *already-known* letters) to each child in a small group. Children would then be asked to quickly sort the magnetic letters into categories (Clay, 2005b): "Put all the Ms in one group, and Ps in another" or "put all the lowercase Ms with an uppercase M as quick as you can." It is helpful to ask children to work quickly when they already know the task. Doing so pushes learners into a faster response that can be more easily accessed and used during reading and writing tasks.

Teachers, however, should not ask for a fast response when a letter, word, or concept is still new or challenging (Clay, 2005b). If a child is likely to reverse a letter, requiring a fast response will increase the odds that this reversal will occur again and thus become habituated. This difficulty is normal in children's development and occurs particularly from one context to another. A child learning a new letter will begin with slow, laborious thinking and problem solving. She has to learn both this new letter, and its relationship to other, already-known letters (Clay, 2001). A child might continue to have difficulty attending to the same letter within a different word or when reading a word that begins with a letter known only for writing. It is likely, then, that children will make errors even when a letter has become relatively well known.

Differentiated Instruction for Foundational Skills.

The sequence used for instruction in foundational skills should be adjusted over time for optimal learning. Some letters or words are more difficult to learn than others, both because of their characteristics and children's learning histories. Emergent readers may not yet pay automatic attention to spatial orientation and directionality in print, for example, and can become confused when asked to learn the letters *b* and *d* together. It is important, in this case, to teach either *b* or *d* first and not introduce the related letter until initial learning has become firm. Similarly, if a child is already showing difficulties with particular words (perhaps confusing the words *like* and *look*), then teaching another similar word (such as *let*) may increase the child's confusion. Likewise, attempting to teach the word *the* to an emergent reader who is new to English may be more difficult than would the word *cat*. Although *the* is a very useful, high-frequency word, it is less concrete and may be less easily understood and remembered.

Teachers should incorporate review within lessons to help children expand, consolidate, and integrate new knowledge. Andrew, for example, decided to incorporate a quick reteaching of the new word practiced in a recent skills lesson prior to his group's reading lesson. He did so after observing that students in this group were continuing to make errors on this word while reading:

> You learned the word *my* this morning. Think about what *my* looks like [showing the word on a whiteboard for students' use as needed]. Say *my* slowly, and think about how this word sounds. Write the word in the air with your fingers and say it to yourself.
>
> Now look in your book and find the word *my*. When your finger points here [the word *my*] you have to say "my." Let's read together: I see my house. Read it by yourself and make sure that what you read looks right.

Foundational Skills in Context

Children who know particular letters and words in isolation may not be able to use this information when reading and writing text. A child, for example, may recognize the word *go* accurately during classroom word wall practice, yet still read the word incorrectly in text. Clay (2001, 2005a) advocated, then, for a careful balance between instruction on item knowledge (letter/ letter sound and word identification) and guided practice using these same foundational skills when comprehending and producing written text. Otherwise, children may become so focused on individual letters or words that they ignore language and meaning while reading. Neglect of these essential sources of information blocks children's progress and limits learning to an unnecessarily slow and laborious pace. This occurs when children are not given opportunities "to conduct the orchestra" (Clay, 2014, p. 221)—to pull information from all sources together to read for themselves. Reading large amounts of continuous text builds proficiency in matching sound sequences (phonemic awareness) to print (Clay, 2005b). A child who has lots of opportunities to read and write the high-frequency word *look*, for example, internalizes a match between how the word sounds and how it looks in print. This expectation for how a word should look in print supports children's self-monitoring and the ability to learn other, related words.

Emergent readers will use low-level strategies as a starting point for their reading, responding to pictures and matching their speech to memory of a familiar text (Clay, 2001). As they learn to cross-check one source of information with another, however, their use of all sources of information starts to become more sophisticated (Clay, 2005b). Andrew demonstrated one-to-one, word-by-word matching for his students, for example, after introducing the easy book *I Like to Eat* (Siamon, 1992). As he read the sentence *I like to eat*, he pointed word-by-word and inserted the additional word *everything*: "I like to eat everything." Andrew then demonstrated monitoring for his students ("I ran out of words; I'll try that again"), and reread the sentence correctly. Next, Andrew asked his students to point to several known words within the text: "Find the word *I*. Find the word *to*." He pointed and read the sentence again, pausing briefly on the words *I* and *to* for emphasis. Finally, Andrew listened as children in the group read the new book independently, and prompted as needed: "Did that match? Were there enough words? Did you run out of words?" (Clay, 2005b, p. 106).

LEARNING CONCEPTS ABOUT PRINT

Children learn how to look at print as they (1) follow the rules for directionality in English, (2) see and understand spaces or word boundaries, and (3) understand the concepts of a letter and a word (Clay, 2001, 2005b). Teachers should expect large differences in how well individual children pay attention to print as they begin formal literacy instruction. Young children, for example, do not automatically attend to print in a left-to-right, top-to-bottom direction. Kindergarten and 1st-grade children may not yet use a consistent starting point on the page when reading or writing, or know how to control their visual search left-to-right across letters within a word (Clay, 2005b). Such difficulties are a normal part of young children's development and should not be viewed as evidence of a reading disability. Most children, in fact, confuse similar-looking letters or words while learning to read, and research demonstrates that reading disabilities "do *not* result from visual problems producing letter and word reversals" (International Literacy Association, 2016, p. 2). Instead, children differ in their early interest in environmental print and storybook reading, and may not have had sufficient opportunities to understand how people access and create written language. Most young readers simply need finely tuned, differentiated instruction to establish correct directional habits (Clay, 2005b).

Teaching Concepts About Print

Crisp and deliberate teacher demonstration is vital for teaching concepts about print. Teachers' verbal attempts to explain concepts about print for young learners are likely to cause confusion. This is particularly true for the left-to-right and top-to-bottom directional rules of English, and for complex ideas such as what a word is or where a period should be placed. Children do not learn foundational skills simply by being told what to do (Clay, 2005b). Telling children, for example, to put a period (or other ending punctuation) at the end of each sentence is not effective. Instead, children need instruction that demonstrates how such skills are put into practice.

Shared Reading. Shared reading lessons (Holdaway, 1984) are taught in both whole-class and small-group contexts, and they are an excellent interactive context for learning concepts about print. The overall goal of shared reading lessons is to establish children's interest in a wide variety of challenging narrative stories, informational texts, and poetry, while also teaching for comprehension, language skills, decoding strategies, fluency, and concepts about print.

Shared reading lessons provide multiple opportunities for students to become fluent, enthusiastic readers. Children hear and read a new text multiple times across several shared reading lessons. These stories should be displayed in a clear format so that all students can see the text without strain. (Children's visual systems for reading are still developing. Projecting a dimly lighted, fuzzy text in a small text size such that children must angle their heads awkwardly, or try to see text through glare, does not work.) Texts should be read several times within each lesson, using teacher read-aloud, choral, or echo reading. Rereadings increase the amount of time spent in sustained reading and improve children's fluency. The teacher should always read these texts proficiently—with enthusiasm, good expression, accuracy, and fluency.

The teacher will briefly demonstrate concepts about print for children, using two or three of the teaching activities listed in Figure 2.1 based on children's most immediate needs.

The teacher should address any areas of concern, perhaps providing demonstration or explanation if students are not solving words effectively, or reviewing one or two previously taught letters. Andrew, for example, observed signs that his students were not yet distinguishing between letters and words. He began, then, to point precisely and use the terms *letter* and *word* very deliberately during sharing reading: "Oh, I made a mistake on that *word*. It doesn't make sense. I need to look carefully at the first *letter* in the *word*, S, and read the sentence again."

The teacher will also lead a 5- to 10-minute discussion in each lesson to develop children's understanding of the text. This teaching might address character traits, or text structure (events within a narrative, main ideas and supporting details in informational text, or a rhyme structure in poetry). Although the overall time for shared reading lessons is limited (no more than 20–25 minutes per lesson), expanding children's text comprehension is still essential.

Prompting for Children's Use of Concepts About Print. Teachers need to remain alert to children's lingering confusions as they read and write text (Clay, 2005b). Children who do not yet use a consistent starting point at the top left of the page, for example, are in need of clear, immediate prompting. During a small-group reading lesson, a teacher can simply point to the correct place to start on a page just before a child begins to read independently. This activity will help a child develop the habit of beginning to read and write from a top-left position. When a child has skipped a word in text, the teacher might simply reread up to the error while pointing word by word (without unnecessary teacher talk). The prompting is quick and targeted, and allows the child to return quickly to sustained reading. These on-the-spot reminders ensure that confusions and challenges are not practiced incorrectly. Otherwise, such problems become increasingly difficult to correct over time (Clay, 2005b).

LEARNING LETTERS

Readers must know *what* to look for in print, *where* to look for needed information, and *which way* to look across print (Kaye & Lose, 2015). This includes noticing and using letters and letter sequences from left to right

Figure 2.1. Teaching Concepts About Print During Shared Reading

Skill	Activity	Explanation
Top, Left-Hand Starting Point	Point to the first word in text as reading begins.	Crisp demonstration without unneeded teacher talk.
One-to-One Matching	Use pointer to match one-to-one while reading a short section of text.	Crisp word-by-word pointing (not sliding).
Return Sweep	Use pointer to demonstrate return sweep from one line to the next.	Do not overdo, causing unnecessary line-by-line pausing.
Letter/Sound Knowledge	"What letter do you expect to see at the beginning of *stop*?" (Clay, 2005b, p. 108)	Use the term *letter* clearly, and point to the first letter in the word.
Left to Right Across a Word	Draw card across a word, showing one letter at a time while articulating sounds slowly.	Do not pronounce sounds in separated fashion. Say the word normally with slow articulation.
Punctuation	Use verbal punctuation: "She was very frightened, exclamation point!"	Avoid complex explanation of punctuation.

within words. Over time, children learn many aspects of letter knowledge in detail and with fast production (see Figure 2.2). Children are then able to choose the most efficient way to access and use letter knowledge while reading and writing, without being limited to a narrow range of letter knowledge.

Teaching for Comprehensive Letter Knowledge

Teachers need to be able to correctly interpret children's responses during instruction. The child, for example, who names the letter *M* as "Mom" has demonstrated useful, initial knowledge via a matching keyword. A child who identifies a letter by reciting the alphabet up to that letter also has at least one way to address the task. Of course, neither of these early strategies is sufficient for long-term literacy gains. Any accurate knowledge that a child already has about a letter, however, serves as a good starting point.

Teaching letters primarily within whole-class lessons, using a routine schedule of one letter per week or in alphabetic sequence, is not the best use of classroom time (Jones & Reutzel, 2012; McKay & Teale, 2015). Children who have limited exposure to storybooks and print, and virtually no known letters, for instance, will benefit from an early focus on easy-to-learn letters (perhaps *X, O,* and *S*; letters in words they already know; or letters at the beginning of their own first names). It is also crucial to reserve time across the

Figure 2.2. Learning About Letters

Concept About Print	Letter Knowledge
Concept of Letter	Letters are different from words (even though a few words have only one letter).
Letter Formation	Writing a letter requires a particular set of hand and arm movements.
	Letters have a required orientation; most cannot be reversed.
Letter Identification	Letters have their own names, visual forms, sounds, and key words.
	Even small differences in form matter (such as the difference between *t* and *f*).
	Uppercase letters do not always have the same shape as the matching lowercase letter.
Letter Sound Identification	Sounds are associated with letters and combinations of letters (but many sounds can be represented with varying letters or letter combinations).
Phonemic Awareness	A sequence of letter sounds can be articulated and heard within words, and used for spelling and decoding decisions.

school year for intentional and systematic instruction on letters as needed. Teaching one letter *per day*, starting at the beginning of the school year, can result in stronger achievement than does a schedule of one letter per week (Jones & Reutzel, 2012). This initial, 26-day cycle introduces all children quickly to the full set of letters and leaves time for additional, purposeful teaching. Children who already know most letters have early opportunities to learn new ones, and students who know few letters encounter many examples they can use to understand what a letter is and how to approach this new learning (Jones & Reutzel, 2012). Additional cycles across the rest of the school year can focus on review of letters (as needed) that are (a) visually similar, (b) particularly interesting to children, (c) related to themed studies in science or art, or (d) more difficult to learn. Andrew decided, for example, that the students in his reading group needed to strengthen their knowledge of about 10 highly useful and easy-to-learn letters. He began with a 5-minute lesson on the letters *S*, *M*, and *T*, rearranging the lowercase magnetic letters for each question and pointing carefully:

> I'll say the names of these letters: *S*, *M*, *T*. Raise your hand if your name begins with *T*. With *S*. With *M*. Name each letter quickly with me: *T*, *S*, *M*. Margie, come up and point to the letter *T*. Good!

Everyone, write a lowercase *t* on your whiteboard five times. Carrie, point to the letter that the word *Mom* starts with. Good! Everyone, write a lowercase *M* five times. Sarah, point to the letter that your name starts with. Yes! Write a lowercase *S* five times. Now, write each letter one time on your whiteboard. When I say the letter's name, point to it and say it with me.

Lessons for letter learning should provide explicit teacher demonstration and explanation for what students are expected to learn, avoiding a reliance on macaroni, costumes, or songs for teaching letters (McKay & Teale, 2015). A lesson might start with a direct statement from the teacher telling the letter's name, shape, and associated sound(s). (It is counterproductive to first ask students to state this information themselves. Questions such as "What do you think this letter is?" too often result in inaccurate or off-topic responses and may muddle the expected learning.) After brief teacher explanation, children are asked to say the letter name, identify keywords or names that start with that letter, write the letter, read words from the classroom word wall that start with the letter, or hunt for the letter within familiar, easy text. They can practice letters orally, by drawing in the air or on small whiteboards, and by reciting and explaining letter knowledge to a partner.

Writing Letters. Writing is a slower process than reading, requiring children to attend to the details of print in ways they may not do when reading (Clay, 2001, 2014). When building messages in print, children must construct even the smallest segments of print (using features of letters, spaces between words, and upper/lowercase letterforms) while also organizing information in words and sentences. Writing, then, fosters slow analysis of the details of written text, draws attention to letterforms and sequences, and requires coordination of different sources of knowledge (Clay, 2014).

It is difficult for children to simply look at a new letter and remember it in all of its detail. Writing, however, brings letter learning within children's reach by integrating movement with complex learning. This is crucial as children learn how to distinguish between visually (*n* and *m*) and auditorily similar (*d* and *g*) letters. Teachers can help students by providing a verbal description to use while forming a letter. This language describes the *movement* needed for a letter (Clay, 2005b). To form the letter *e*, for example, a verbal description such as "straight over, up, and around" may work well. Describing the letter *b* as "a stick and then a circle" tells what the letter *b* looks like and is less effective than describing the movement required by pencil, hand, and arm to form the letter: "Down, up, and around." With repetition across several short lessons, children internalize the letterform and verbal description, and are sometimes heard whispering the directions to themselves as a self-scaffold. Once a verbal description has been established for a particular letter, the teacher can lean in while children write independently and prompt as needed. To help a child remember how to write the letter *t*, for example, a teacher might say, "Start here, go down, and across."

Alphabet Books. Individual daily practice reciting a very simple ABC book is helpful for children who are still learning letters (Clay, 2005b). These books highlight one letter per page, using one upper- and one low-ercase letter along with a matching picture. Letters are printed in an easy-to-find location on the page, and in easy-to-read font style, color, and size. Teachers should carefully examine the pictures to determine suitability for early letter practice: Will children be able to correctly identify what each picture represents? Is the picture a good example of the letter's sound? Ex-amples of published ABC books that may work for this purpose include *26 Letters and 99 Cents* (Hoban, 1987) and *John Burningham's ABC* (Burning-ham, 1964). Teachers may also want to construct their own ABC books for particular children, using simple, stapled books and stickers.

Children should practice reading their alphabet book each day from A to Z, pointing as they recite the letter name and keyword: "A, A, apple." This reading should be as fluent as possible, and the teacher should quickly supply a correct letter name or label for a picture whenever a child makes an error or hesitates. This prompting is done without explanation, so the child can quickly continue reading. Practice with ABC books occurs in small-group instruction, with partners, or individually with a classroom volunteer. Children develop a well-practiced access to letter knowledge for letterforms, sounds, and keywords with frequent, daily rehearsal.

The teacher can then use the ABC book as a prompt to help a child during reading and writing lessons (Clay, 2005b). If a child, for example, needs to write the letter *r* but has difficulty remembering it, the teacher ei-ther shows the relevant page from the book as a reference or asks the child to access memory: "R, R, rabbit. What does that letter look like in your ABC book?"

Teacher Prompting for Letter Use While Reading. When teachers tell children to "sound out" a difficult word, they expect them to engage in the complex, sequential process described in Figure 2.3. This process encom-passes a more difficult and complex set of tasks than might be anticipated. A child may not know the correct sound for a particular letter. Or, after articulating the sounds seen within a word, a child may still not recognize the word. It is particularly difficult for children to identify a word when it has been articulated with an "uh" sound for each letter; articulating the word *fast* as "fuh ă suh tuh" makes the word quite difficult to puzzle out.

Figure 2.3. "Sounding Out" as Complex Decisionmaking

	Child's Actions	Needed Knowledge
1	Search the letters from left to right across the word.	Understand which printed form is a letter and which is a word. Identify a word by finding a space before and after it in print. Know where to find the beginning of the word and which direction to look next.
2	Identify and assign a sound to each letter.	Know the sounds associated with each letter. (Sounds vary; children may need to try an alternate sound.)
3	Determine when a combination of letters should be articulated.	Know how letter combinations (such as *sh* or *oi*) should be pronounced.
4	Articulate and blend each sound.	Know how to blend sounds in sequence, without adding "uh," distorting, or separating sounds.
5	Use these sounds to identify a known word, state the resulting word, and continue reading.	Able to connect the blended sounds to a meaningful, known word.

Fortunately, additional sources of information are available that make decoding unfamiliar words easier and more developmentally friendly (Schwartz, 2015). As children detect errors while reading, they gradually learn how to use information from letter sounds and a text's meaning. Clay (2005b), for example, recommended specific prompting language during reading instruction to shape children's word decoding:

- Where is the first letter?
- What is a word that starts with that letter?
- Does this help? [Pointing to a helpful cue] (pp. 203–204)

Clay (2005b) recommended prompting that directs children to letters and sounds along with language structures and meaning: "What would make sense, and sound right and look like that?" (p. 205). When a child in his reading group stopped and showed signs of uncertainty after misreading the word *Mom* as *Dad*, for example, Andrew initiated a useful prompting conversation:

Andrew: Would Dad start like that?

Child: No, it looks wrong.

Andrew: Right! Look at this part [the M in *Mom*]. Does that help?

Child: I know, /m/. Mom?

Andrew: Run your finger under the word and say *Mom* slowly. Does it look like Mom?

Child: [articulates the word *Mom* slowly] Yes!

Andrew: So what can you try now?

Child: Read it again?

Andrew: Try that, and see if *Mom* makes sense and looks right.

Andrew, then, directed the child's attention to a known initial consonant, and asked him to confirm his error correction using both phonetic and meaning-based information. This interaction represents teaching to a multiple action chain (McGee, Kim, Nelson, & Fried, 2015) and demonstrates the child's growing ability to consider both letter sounds and decoding as well as language and meaning. Children should not be encouraged to simply skip difficult words when reading text for instructional purposes. Although there are some possible exceptions to this principle (for occasional complex and unfamiliar proper nouns or technical vocabulary, for example), students generally need to practice using strategic activity as they work to identify challenging words—coming as close as possible to a correct and meaningful word given their current skills.

SUMMARY

Clay's conceptualization of teaching as adaptive expertise is one of the legacies of her work (McNaughton, 2014). Experts focus instruction on clear goals, and they are intentional and strategic. Expert teachers engage in problem solving and implement solutions based on observation of student responses within classroom contexts. In this chapter, we have presented examples of one kindergarten teacher's expansion into effective instructional practices when teaching foundational skills. Andrew used systematic observation and running records to identify key roadblocks to his students' progress and used this information to design needed instruction. His revised and expanded instruction for this group of students supported their use of strategic activity (in place of their attempts to simply memorize texts):

- Taught students how to study new words to support their early monitoring during text reading

- Reviewed newly taught words prior to small-group reading lessons to direct students' attention to a known part of print for easier monitoring and self-correction
- Demonstrated and provided practice for students' monitoring with one-to-one matching while reading
- Used the terms *letter* and *word* precisely, with clear pointing during instruction to increase children's understanding of these concepts
- Provided differentiated letter instruction to establish students' strong knowledge for a small group of letters before proceeding with instruction on additional letters
- Prompted for students' integrated use of both phonetic and meaning-based information during text reading to monitor, search for information, and self-correct.

FURTHER STUDY

Clay, M. M. (2000b). *Concepts about print: What have children learned about the way we print language?* Portsmouth, NH: Heinemann.

Study the information in this book with colleagues to understand how children learn concepts about print and how this knowledge is assessed. Practice administering Clay's *Concepts About Print* observation task with colleagues, and consider the kinds of information about students' progress that would be most helpful for teaching decisions. Next, administer this observation task to a few children, analyzing the results and considering what teaching is needed.

Pressley, M., Allington, R. L., Wharton-MacDonald, R., Collins-Block, C., & Morrow, L. M. (2001). Andy Schultheis. In *Learning to read: Lessons from exemplary first-grade classrooms* (pp. 101–128). New York, NY: Guilford.

Read this chapter to find out how one exemplary 1st-grade teacher implemented skill-based lessons integrated with children's authentic reading and writing activities. Consider how the activities described in this chapter might be implemented in your own classroom or school, and construct an initial plan to do so.

CHAPTER 3

The Role of Meaning and Comprehension in Learning
Narrative Text

Meaning is the "given" in all reading—"the source of anticipation, the guide to being on track, and the outcome and reward of the effort" (Clay, 1991a, pp. 1–2). Each time they read, children learn new vocabulary and language, apply knowledge in new ways to decode and understand text, and learn the foundational skills needed for faster and easier monitoring and solving. Reading thus extends children's knowledge, facility with foundational skills, and effective use of strategic activity.

The following sections describe (1) the role of meaning and comprehension in literacy learning, and (2) how comprehension of narrative text is taught through effective conversation and teacher prompting so that children learn how to anticipate text structure and use comprehension strategies. We begin with an illustration of teaching for comprehension in a small-group reading lesson. The following focus questions will help readers anticipate key topics while reading this chapter:

1. Why is children's text comprehension, including their ability to monitor for and maintain meaning while reading, crucial for overall literacy development?
2. When is the best time to begin comprehension instruction for young children?
3. What role do teacher-provided introductions for new and challenging texts play in children's learning?
4. Are children who monitor their reading primarily for letter sound and word reading accuracy, or who often skip or simply sound out difficult words one letter at a time, likely to make good progress in reading proficiency?
5. What do teachers need to know in order to implement powerful instructional conversations with students?
6. Why is children's copying of graphic organizers during whole class discussion not sufficient for learning how to anticipate meaning and text structure?

7. What types of teacher questions best help children develop strong comprehension skills?

INTEGRATED DECODING AND COMPREHENSION INSTRUCTION

Julie began her teaching of a 1st-grade, small-group reading lesson with explanation of a decoding strategy: "When you come to a word you don't know, look for parts to help yourself figure it out." Julie slid a card from left to right to uncover the parts of the word *vacation* (*va ca tion*; written on a small whiteboard). She then helped students locate the word in their new reading book, and asked them to articulate parts in the word slowly while sliding their own finger under the word. Next, Julie introduced her students to the new book *Just One Guinea Pig* (Giles, 1997):

> You're doing a great job learning how to understand characters and events in a story. You're going to practice these again today in a new book. In this story, Laura's parents tell her that she can't have her own guinea pig. What do you think she will do?

After a brief discussion of their predictions, Julie's students were ready to read: "While you read, think about what you need to know about the characters to understand the story." As her students read independently, Julie observed each child for signs of monitoring. She noticed, for example, that one of her students paused and then smiled while rereading the description of the guinea pig's (Mop's) long white hair: "She looks like a little floor mop." Julie also leaned in briefly and used a card to help another child look for parts in the difficult word *everyone*.

When each student had read the story at least once, Julie asked her students to understand what each of the characters said when they saw Mop's babies: "Robert and Mom sound happy and surprised, don't they? What did they say?" Next, Julie asked her students to turn to a partner and talk about what Dad and Laura said on this same page, and what they think the author wanted them to understand about these characters. As Julie listened in on the partner conversations, however, she observed that her students had not used textual details effectively for strong answers to this question. Consequently, she directed her students to reread and decide what information the author wanted them to notice:

> *Julie:* Think carefully about what the author told you. What did Dad say when he saw the baby guinea pigs?
> *Student 1:* He saw the four babies.

Student 2: He said, "Oh, no!"
Julie: Yes. How does that help you understand how Dad was feeling?
Student 3: He's not happy.
Student 2: He didn't like them too much. There are too many now.
Julie: Right. So he is a bit upset about so many more guinea pigs. Why do you think this might worry him?

Julie then asked the group to reread the last page in the book and describe how the characters reacted to the last event in the story (adopting one of Mop's new babies). As her students responded, Julie asked them to read a phrase from the text to prove their thinking. Finally, the group read this last page chorally: "Make your voices show what Dad and Laura are thinking":

> "All right," said Dad.
> "But just **one** guinea pig."
> "Oh, Moppet," smiled Laura,
> "I can keep you." (Giles, 1997, p. 16)

This reading lesson took approximately 20 minutes. Julie taught decoding, comprehension, and fluency (accuracy, pace, phrasing, and language-like expression). She focused on students' close attention to understanding the text, and avoided any lengthy discussion on topics not directly related to the text's main ideas or theme. She utilized her students' brief partner talk as formative assessment, and accordingly provided further explanation on how readers understand characters' response to events. She was, then, teaching her students how to build an accurate and coherent understanding of the author's meanings on both literal and inferential levels.

Teachers provide an orientation to new texts as a framework to guide young readers through successful processing of information (Clay, 2014). Julie named and demonstrated learning goals for students, and she provided a purpose for their thinking while they read. Such teaching scaffolds children's learning by enlisting their interests, highlighting relevant features of the task, avoiding frustration, and demonstrating new skills (Wood, Bruner, & Ross, 1976). Instructional scaffolding, then, does not *protect* children from complex issues or texts. Instead, scaffolding ensures that children *can* tackle appropriately challenging tasks successfully.

Beginning readers need to be familiar with the ideas, plot, and language in a new book used for instruction (Clay, 2005b). Teachers and students, then, engage in a brief conversation before reading about story elements, language, unusual names, and main ideas of a new text as needed.

Although teacher and students may review and discuss portions of the text or pictures, this instruction is much more complex than any simple "picture walk." The teacher does not read the book to students first, nor does the teacher simply review a list of words. Teacher introductions to new texts are provided at differing levels of support, depending on the degree of challenge in the new book and children's current reading knowledge. Some children need a highly supportive teacher introduction to a new text, with a significant amount of information provided by the teacher before reading, and others only a minimal introduction. If there are only one or two children in a group who need a highly supportive book introduction, the teacher might provide this for them as pre-teaching prior to the small group lesson. On the other hand, if students can decode and comprehend the new text without the assistance of a teacher-provided introduction, then the text is most likely not a good choice for their reading instruction. Instead, students can read the text independently and should read more challenging texts during instruction.

READING NARRATIVE TEXT FOR ENJOYMENT AND UNDERSTANDING

Narrative texts use storytelling structures to entertain and inform: a narrative problem, characters' actions and events, and a resolution. The elements of narrative texts are generally familiar to teachers (setting, voice, characters, episodes, and plot), and storytelling is central to all human cultures. Most children settle in quickly, for example, and listen avidly to any engaging story told orally or read aloud. It is misleading, in fact, to assume that narrative text does not expand readers' knowledge. Narrative text teaches children how people may feel and act in light of particular problems, or how they interact with one another and the world. Patricia Polacco's *The Keeping Quilt* (1996), for instance, teaches about the joys of family, heritage, art, and human communities. Children construct knowledge within narrative texts through their understanding of complex and important themes: friendship, tragedy, or the power of an individual's commitment to positive values, for example. Building children's ability to comprehend narrative texts, then, remains essential (along with children's reading and writing of informational text).

Clay (2001) defined strategic activity as in-the-head thinking and problem solving. Children work to (1) pick up information from print, language, and meaning; (2) understand and use that information to make a decision about their reading; and then (3) monitor whether their response is a good fit (Clay, 1991a). Readers' strategic activity is driven both by the text itself and the reader's background knowledge and purpose for reading, leading to the construction of meaning (Kucer, 2014). As children begin to take control over strategies used to understand text, they learn not only *what* should be attended to while reading but *how* to do so as well. Comprehension-building strategies include children's

- purposeful use of what they know to understand characters and events, and to predict what events might occur next,
- ability to ask their own questions about the story in order to understand it in more detail,
- construction of a mental image of the plot or events,
- monitoring whether they understand what they are reading, and use of rereading or other "fix it" strategies to repair comprehension as needed,
- use of knowledge of the world to understand inferences, and
- monitoring and rehearsal of comprehension by summarizing story elements and considering the author's theme.

TEACHING FOR MEANING AND COMPREHENSION

Comprehension and decoding competencies must be taught together from the beginning of literacy instruction (Clay, 2001; National Institute of Child Health and Human Development, 2000; Shanahan, Callison, Carriere, Duke, Pearson, Schatschneider, & Torgesen, 2010). All children must learn how to comprehend at increasingly sophisticated levels of understanding, beginning when they are still learning how to decode text. The old adage advising that children learn to read first and then read to learn is incorrect (e.g., Houck & Ross, 2012; Robb, 2002). There is no point in time when children should not be reading (and listening to texts read aloud) for enjoyment, understanding, and information. Even a very simple emergent reading book should be well constructed, with a plot and characters for beginning readers to consider. *I Can Read* (Malcolm, 1983), for example, is a very early, short reading text for emergent readers. It is written with a repeating language structure that scaffolds emergent readers and allows them to practice matching words in print to speech and identify a few key, high-frequency words. The text tells the story of a young girl who reads not only to family and friends, but also proudly to herself: "I can read to my friend. I can read to myself!" (Malcolm, 1983, p. 7–8).

The need for simultaneous, ongoing instruction in both foundational skills and comprehension is validated by the observed characteristics of proficient and less proficient readers. Proficient, beginning readers demonstrate a strong, overriding concern for meaning (Kucer, 2014). They build meaning by integrating information in text with background knowledge. Less proficient readers, on the other hand, fail to notice when what they have read does not make sense (and thus do not use strategies to fix their comprehension). Less proficient readers resort to sounding out or skipping words (rather than rereading or parsing out ideas from the text) when they monitor a lack of understanding (Kucer, 2014). Less proficient readers lack sufficient understanding of meaning-getting strategies. Crucially, then, less proficient readers do not consistently read for meaning and are likely to suffer the consequences of this deficiency throughout school literacy tasks and as they attempt to explore personal interests through text.

Clay's research (1982, 2001) demonstrated that high-progress readers learn how to coordinate multiple sources of information through monitoring, searching for more information, and self-correction processes. Children, for example, are not simply guessing when they use meaning as a source of information while reading. Instead, as children monitor whether a word or sentence has made sense, this active thinking sends them in search of additional information from letters, words, language, and meaning. These processes result in children's increasingly sophisticated use of all sources of information in an integrated manner when reading text (Clay, 1991a). Clay (2005b) recommended prompting children for their use of sources of information: "You said . . . Does that make sense?" or "What would make sense, and sound right and look like that?" (p. 205). U.S. national reviews of research, including the National Reading Panel (National Institute of Child Health and Human Development, 2000), Preventing Reading Difficulties (Snow, Burns, & Griffin, 1998), and studies of the instructional practices of exemplary teachers (e.g., Taylor, Pearson, Clark, & Walpole, 2000; Wharton-McDonald, Pressley, & Hampston, 1998) have also identified the need for children's integrated learning of both comprehension and decoding.

The following sections illustrate specific aspects of teachers' effective interaction with students during comprehension instruction, including an illustration of both poor- and high-quality literacy discussion, teaching for understanding of narrative text structure, and the characteristics of teachers' questions. We also provide a description of Discussion Web (Alvermann, 1991), an activity that engages children in structured conversation with peers about text comprehension.

Interactive Read-Aloud and Teacher Questioning

Teachers routinely ask children questions about what they have read. All too often, however, this teacher questioning does little to show children *how* to comprehend. The following example of a read-aloud discussion occurred after the book *Miss Rumphius* (Cooney, 1982) was read to students in a whole-class setting. This beautiful, touching story is told from the viewpoint of Miss Rumphius's grandniece, who describes how Miss Rumphius (named Alice) planted lupines throughout her small town. In the example below, however, the teacher simply asked a series of literal questions:

> **Teacher:** What were the two things that Alice wanted to do in her life? Anna?
> **Anna:** Oh, travel places, and live by the sea.
> **Teacher:** Right! Where did she travel? Yes, Tim?
> **Tim:** A, a fishing village, and with a camel.
> **Teacher:** Yes. What were those places called?
> **Anna:** With Bapa Raja and kangaroos?
> **Teacher:** Okay. She went to a fishing village, to tall mountains, and the Land of the Lotus-Eaters. What did Miss Rumphius do after she got old?
> **Leticia:** She planted all the flowers.

It is all too easy to assume that this lesson might improve students' reading comprehension skills. Basal teaching manuals, in fact, routinely recommend this type of after-reading questioning. No actual instruction took place in this example, however. The teacher did not attempt to improve children's thinking, even when their responses were not fully on target. The teacher also did not explain or demonstrate *how* information was obtained or inferred from the text, and did not stretch students' comprehension to inferential or application levels of understanding. The few students who responded probably found it easy to comprehend the story on their own and at the level required by the questions. It is not likely that children in the class developed improved knowledge or stronger comprehension because of this activity.

In contrast, interactive read-aloud lessons utilize carefully constructed teacher and student dialogue that promotes in-depth understanding of content and effective strategies. Teachers will direct students' attention to inferential information and ideas during discussion, and listen carefully to the quality of their responses. This approach results in more effective conversation with students and a more detailed understanding of children's skills and knowledge. The instructional excerpt below illustrates several ways in which children's active participation in strong comprehension instruction might be structured after the reading of *Miss Rumphius*. (Each child had a small whiteboard to record responses on, and the text was displayed on a document camera during the discussion.)

Teacher: I love that story! What kind of person do you think Miss Rumphius was?

Carrie: She's pretty. And old too.

Kenny: She was nice to everyone.

Teacher: I think so too. Think about this question: What did it say in the story to make us know that she was kind? Make a quick picture on your whiteboard to show how we know that Miss Rumphius was kind. [After 1 minute] Suzie, what did you draw?

Suzie: She helped people.

Teacher: Good detail, Suzie. You made a picture of the library she worked in. Read that part of the story to us.

Suzie: [Reading] There she worked in a library, dusting books and keeping them from getting mixed up, and helping people find the ones they wanted.

Kenny: And this part, too. The Bapa Raja gave her a shell and said she would always be his heart.

Caroline: But they called her the Crazy Old Lady. Weren't they afraid of her?

James: But not . . . after, they called her the Flower Lady.

Teacher: Let's think about that a bit more. It might help us to understand if we review what the end of the story said about Miss Rumphius. Turn to your partner and help each other decide if people were frightened of her, or if they thought she was nice. Tell your partner what happened in the story to make you think so.

All children had opportunities to participate in this discussion. Engagement occurred through drawing and by talking with peers, and not just in response to teacher questions. The teacher began the discussion by posing an inferential question about the larger meaning of the text and directed students back to the text to support their thinking. Interesting and important details from the text were discussed during the lesson as needed in order to infer information and respond to the story's theme.

Reading wonderful stories aloud to children increases their immersion in entertaining and inspiring literature, and promotes a lifelong love of reading. Story reading sessions can address a variety of purposes and goals. Teachers may choose to read a story or poem to children simply for their enjoyment. Such activities are valuable and serve to expand children's language and world knowledge. Interactive read-aloud sessions, however, are a teaching opportunity. Teachers encourage children to talk about the text, while avoiding lengthy discussions about connections or personal experiences that are only vaguely related to the text's big ideas. It would not have improved students' comprehension, for example, if they had named all the other books they knew with flowers in them before hearing *Miss Rumphius*. The point of interactive read-aloud instruction is not simply to have children talk about whatever occurs easily to them, but to direct their talk in ways that are most productive for learning. Teachers, for example, can demonstrate any thinking needed to understand the text or provide details as needed in support of children's accurate and insightful reasoning about the information in texts.

Instruction during teacher interactive read-aloud provides strong opportunities for children to learn content knowledge, vocabulary, and comprehension. Children must also practice these skills in their own reading of texts. Otherwise, they do not learn how to integrate their own search for information across letters, words, language, and information while reading.

Learning to Anticipate Narrative Text Structure

Children's improved understanding of narrative text structure is an important instructional goal. They need to be able to anticipate plot, identify story elements, and understand the use of literary language. In this section, we illustrate important principles needed for two general approaches to teaching narrative text structure: guided retelling and graphic organizers.

Guided Retelling. Guided retelling engages children in holistic comprehension; the task causes learners to relate one part of the story to another as the retelling proceeds (Morrow, 1996). Children are guided in their re-creation of story elements and plot by a series of questions (see Figure 3.1).

Children can use these questions (modified as needed to match how text structure has been discussed in instruction) as prompts to orally retell a story with a partner or small group of three or four children. The prompts are displayed during retelling practice, perhaps on the document viewer or attached inside the covers of a file folder. Or, children can draw each part of the story (perhaps the setting, characters, and series of events) and use their drawings to prompt retelling. It is helpful to provide a list of keywords for children to use as they retell. Sequence words (*first, next, last,* or *beginning, middle, end*) can be used by children to describe events in a story, for example, or *at last, finally,* or *the problem was solved when . . .* to describe the story's conclusion. Guided retelling allows children to engage in rich talk and collaboration with peers for improved story comprehension.

Children can also retell stories by constructing a map depicting story elements, drawing a portrait of a character with dialogue bubbles demonstrating the character's motivations or actions, or writing and reading a Readers Theatre script (Sloyer, 1982). For Readers Theatre, children use

Figure 3.1. Questions to Direct Children's Guided Retelling of Narrative Text

Story Elements	Guiding Questions
Setting	Where/when does the story take place?
	How does this setting affect the plot?
Voice	Who is telling the story?
Characters	Who is/are the main character(s)?
	How does characters' thinking, behavior, or dialogue help you to understand the story's theme?
Problem	What do the characters want or need to accomplish in this story?
	What roadblocks do the characters encounter?
Events	What happens first in the story? Next? After that?
	What action do the characters use to try to solve the problem? Do their actions help or complicate the problem?
Solution	Did the main characters need help to solve the problem?
	How was the problem solved? Is the solution a good one?
Theme	What does the author most want you to understand from this story?
	What lesson (or underlying truth) is taught in the story?

their written script of the story and characters' dialogue for a dramatic reading. They do not memorize lines, act, or use costumes or props. Instead, children simply practice reading with good fluency for a meaningful presentation.

Graphic Organizers. Children might also create a graphic organizer in the form of narrative text structure, such as a story map or timeline. Kindergarten students might begin by identifying beginning, middle, and end, whereas 2nd-grade students could describe episodes and resolution with key details. A child who has simply copied a story map during group discussion, however, has most likely not yet learned how to comprehend the events in a story for himself. When children copy, they focus their attention on spelling a word or phrase correctly and on keeping up with the task itself. Children give limited attention in this case to determining the information needed to complete the graphic for themselves. Instead, children need to learn how to use story maps to structure their own thinking about stories.

Initial teacher demonstrations of story map construction are helpful, as long as the teacher explains how to identify and understand the needed information in text: "I need to remember what happens next in the story. It will help if I look in the book for the next part after Miss Rumphius grows up." Children should also work in small groups to design and complete their own representations of narrative plot or story elements. Children first learn what the purposes of story maps are, and then how to create their own. Extending children's practice so that they learn how to discuss the structure of a story with peers, and design their own graphic representation for a story's plot, improves their ability to anticipate story structure. Instead of simply working from a story map prepared in the whole-class setting, children will have learned how to think about the structure of stories for themselves.

Effective Use of Questioning for Comprehension Instruction

The types of questions constructed by both teachers and children determine the quality of children's thinking about text. Clay (2014) recommended that children be treated as cognitive beings—as learners who are capable of problem solving, expanding their knowledge of language, and understanding relationships between ideas. Children, for instance, tend to become impatient with teachers' "known-answer" questions; they often simply try to figure out what answer the teacher has in mind. Children do not need to be continually tested on their memory of detail level, factual information from a story. Instead, they need to engage in dynamic discussion of interesting and complex questions with both teacher and peers. When children predict the next episode in a story, for example, they also discuss text-based reasons for these predictions. High-level, text-based discussions bring children's attention to understanding what is actually stated or inferred in the text at a deep level. This type of discussion is also more likely to address problems of interest to children's own thinking and experiences.

There are many useful ways to categorize the types of questions asked by teachers. Bloom's Taxonomy (Bloom & Krathwohl, 1956), for example, distinguishes between knowledge, application, analysis, synthesis, and evaluative questions. Literacy standards in general typically call for questions that direct children's attention to inferences, textual details, and central ideas or theme. A focus on three basic types of questions (literal, inferential, and application) is a simple and useful approach (Caldwell, 2008). Teachers should pay particularly close attention to the contrast between literal and inferential questions. Literal questions ask *who, what, where*, or *when* (as long as these are stated explicitly in the text), whereas inferential questions require synthesis of ideas. Inferential questions use language such as *why, how, describe,* or *analyze.* Application questions provide children with opportunities to apply what they have learned from a text to their own lives, using language such as "What might happen if . . ." or "How would you . . ."

When children construct inferential information, they integrate their own knowledge with what is stated in the text to understand an author's intended meaning. In most cases, inferential thinking is required when determining a story's theme, understanding an intended lesson or resolution, or constructing understanding about a character's responses to a story's events. Fountas and Pinnell (2012b) recommend *teaching* students how to infer ("You need to think about what the writer really means but does not say"), *prompting* them to engage in inferential comprehension ("What do you think the writer really meant when he said . . . ?"), and *reinforcing* children's successful inferencing ("You thought about what the writer really meant"; p. 21).

Experience-Text-Relationship. Using Experience-Text-Relationship (Tharp, 1982) questioning ensures that important and interesting questions about text are asked and discussed with children. First, teachers ask students to discuss experiences that are directly related to the text's story elements: "What did it feel like when someone did something nice for you?" Next, children develop general understanding of story elements as they read (or listen to) the text: "How did Miss Rumphius treat the people in her town?" Finally, students are asked to discuss relationships between their own experiences and the text: "What did you learn about being nice to people? What might you do differently at home or at school?" This kind of conversation helps children understand the overall meaning of details as presented in a story and to connect comprehension to their own reasoning, knowledge, and experiences.

Clay (2005b) recommended conversations with children after their reading of a new book, noting that good questions remind children that enjoying and understanding the story is what reading is about. Teachers could initiate conversation in a small-group reading lesson, for example, by asking, "Why do you think Mom and Dad let Laura have a guinea pig after all?" Comprehension-focused conversation, however, should not become an interrogation. Teachers miss opportunities to support children's learning when they ignore their thinking, meanings, or understanding (Clay, 2014). It is also important to teach children how to ask their own questions. Within the conversation depicted above after reading *Miss Rumphius,* for example, the teacher posed a topic and then allowed more than one child to respond before either confirming or redirecting. When a student (Caroline) asked a question, the teacher explicitly valued her contribution and asked students to help explore the issue she raised with evidence from the story's events.

Conversation is a dialogue between two or more speakers; both teacher and children must learn how to communicate through speaking and understand through listening. Teachers, however, bear the responsibility for ensuring that conversations in their classrooms are of high quality and should think of themselves as listeners as much as speakers (Clay, 2014). Effective teachers give children wait time to consider topics and questions, invitations to join in conversations, dialogue exploring what children know about a topic, and the confidence that what they have to say is valued and meaningful (Bennet, 2015).

Discussion Web. Discussion Web (Alvermann, 1991) provides an engaging context to encourage children's active participation in authentic conversations about text. The teacher chooses a text that will be of interest to students and develops a provocative "Yes or No" question for students to consider. The teacher might ask, for example, whether Laura's Dad *really* thinks it's a good idea for her to have her own guinea pig after all. After reading the book, students work in pairs to generate pro and con responses to the question (see Figure 3.2).

Children must not declare for one or the other point of view at this point in the activity. Instead, they should construct reasons to support both a pro and con decision. The teacher can encourage partners to work collaboratively by providing one copy, only, of the chart to each pair.

Next, two sets of partners gather together to compare their reasons for a yes or no decision. They continue to discuss the story in this group of four and try to reach a consensus decision within the group. (It is not necessary for this to be a unanimous decision, however. One or two students might decide on a "minority opinion.") The four students now choose the one reason from their lists that best supports the group's consensus decision.

Figure 3.2. Discussion Web

Does Laura's Dad *really* think it's a good idea
for Laura to have her own guinea pig?

Yes. What happened in the story to make you think so?	No. What happened in the story to make you think so?

Each group of four presents their answer to the whole class along with their choice of a best reason to support their decision. Students can then be asked to write about their own, individual answer, explaining the reasons that best support this decision.

Discussion Web requires students to delve back into the text to identify support for both a yes and a no decision. Students will thus address an interesting high-level question about the text's meaning by revisiting and rehearsing both literal and inferential information with support from peers. The teacher should circulate during these partner and small-group discussions, and ask pertinent questions: "What did it say about that in your story?" or "Why does that make you believe that Dad thinks Laura should not get a guinea pig?" The teacher ensures that individual students are both speaking and listening to others' viewpoints during each phase of the activity.

SUMMARY

The information presented in this chapter is bounded by two key principles. These principles define the nature of reading and children's learning. On the one hand, children's enjoyment in and comprehensive understanding of texts are central to all reading. Without good understanding, reading is not worth doing. Clay (as reported at the beginning of this chapter) described this principle eloquently: Meaning is "the source of anticipation, the guide to being on track, and the outcome and reward of the effort" (1991a, pp. 1–2). Second, literacy instruction honors children as thinkers who can perform complex tasks when provided with appropriate scaffolding—children who are capable of problem solving while reading and writing, and who engage in reasoning and exploration of ideas and information.

In line with these two principles, we presented key points of advice in this chapter for the design and implementation of reading comprehension instruction:

- Do not wait until children are accomplished decoders to begin instruction in reading comprehension.
- Teach decoding and comprehension together and within the context of continuous text.
- Teach comprehension through carefully constructed conversation with children.
- Listen carefully to children's ideas and interests, and encourage them to ask their own questions about text.
- Focus comprehension instruction on strategies. Teach children *how to think* about the information in stories.

- Begin discussions with intriguing inferential- or application-level questions, and then connect the discussion to literal information from text as needed.

FURTHER STUDY

Clay, M. M. (2014). Conversation as one model of teaching interactions. In *By different paths to common outcomes: Literacy learning and teaching* (pp. 13–36). Portsmouth, NH: Heinemann.

> Instructional conversations are central to effective literacy instruction. This very interesting and helpful chapter discusses how teachers negotiate meaning during conversation with children, function effectively as both speaker and listener, and teach in ways that respect children's own thinking and knowledge. After studying this chapter with colleagues, readers might observe (or audio record) an instructional conversation in one another's classrooms, and provide advice and suggestions in light of the information in this chapter.

Clay, M. M. (2014). Introducing storybooks to young readers. In *By different paths to common outcomes: Literacy learning and teaching* (pp. 186–199). Portsmouth, NH: Heinemann.

[Also available as Clay, M. M. (1991). Introducing a new storybook to young readers. *The Reading Teacher, 45*(4), 264–273.]

> This chapter describes specific teaching moves used during the teacher's orientation for young readers to a new book. Clay explains why such introductions are needed for beginning readers, and how introductions support children's learning. Read this chapter to fine-tune small-group, guided reading instruction, and practice a best use of instructional language during reading instruction.

CHAPTER 4

Building Knowledge with Informational Text

Clay (1991a) clearly acknowledged the importance of children's engagement with texts in her work, not only in terms of books but also children's self-created texts from writing: "All of the written texts of the home, the community, the preschool and the school have importance in learning to read" (p. 176). She defined reading as a message-getting, problem-solving activity that could be applied to multiple text types. This problem solving supports children's search through the available information sources in print in order to understand the author's meaning (Clay, 2001; Doyle, 2013). Clay (1991a) also recognized that different text types pose different kinds of problems for young readers to solve.

INCORPORATING INFORMATIONAL TEXTS IN THE CLASSROOM

Teaching practices that help children build knowledge, engage in deeper learning, and maintain a focus on high-order thinking across disciplines are crucial (Partnership for 21st Century Skills, 2013). The Common Core State Standards, for example, recommend that 50% of students' classroom reading material in grades K–5 be informational texts. This goal includes four types of informational texts: (1) literary nonfiction, which combines information with narrative devices like metaphors and descriptive language; (2) expository texts such as textbooks, which present information through description, sequence, cause/effect, problem/solution, and comparison/contrast; (3) persuasive and argumentative texts; and (4) functional/procedural texts, such as directions and recipes, that address steps in a process.

Children's ongoing active reading of continuous texts facilitates their literacy learning (Clay, 1991a, 2001). In addition, learning experiences that combine reading and writing are a benefit to children's acquisition of the language-based knowledge needed to support progress in reading, writing, speaking, and listening. Clay (1991a, 2005a) identified the following forms

61

of information as requisites for becoming literate: knowledge of how the world works; knowledge of letters and words; special features of sound, shape, and layout in text; and special knowledge about books and literary experiences. Furthermore, readers who are making good progress learn how to construct a literacy processing system using all language knowledge sources: "story structure, language structure, words and word structure, letters and the features and sounds of letters" (Doyle, 2013, p. 644).

Although these sources of information are required for understanding any text, certain aspects are uniquely pertinent to children's comprehension of informational texts. For example, to read the informational text *Milk to Ice Cream* (Snyder, 2003) children need to understand the key terms *stir, mixture,* and *ice cream*; comprehend the sequential text structure demonstrating the process of creating ice cream from milk; and understand purposes of text features such as a table of contents and index. These forms of knowledge work together in order for students to comprehend even this simple example of informational text.

In this chapter we explore the role of informational texts for early literacy learning, including knowledge building, critical thinking, problem solving, and comprehension. It will be helpful to consider the following focus questions while reading:

1. How do informational texts build student knowledge?
2. What can teachers do to create curricula that build knowledge?
3. How do thematic units of study contribute to children's literacy learning?
4. What instructional support do children need for collaborative research projects?

BUILDING KNOWLEDGE AND ENLARGING EXPERIENCE

The CCSS recommend an increase in student reading of nonnarrative texts not as a goal unto itself, but as a means to a specific end—the development of student knowledge and deeper thinking around an array of topics:

> By reading texts in history/social studies, science, and other disciplines, students build a foundation of knowledge in these fields that will also give them the background to be better readers in all content areas. (NGACBP & CCSSO, 2010, p. 10)

Clearly, these reading experiences contribute to what Clay referred to as "knowledge of how the world works" (2005a, p. 14), as well as knowledge about vocabulary and books themselves. Clay emphasized that literacy instruction is effective when it provides children with opportunities to use what they already know to build new understandings. Children's prior knowledge includes "all the images, language patterns, social relations, and personal experiences that a student relies on to make sense of something new" (Clay, 2014, p. 248). The expansion of their knowledge base, then, allows children to utilize experiential knowledge, language proficiency, and literacy expertise with more success when reading and writing (Clay, 2001).

Developing students' content knowledge should be on the agenda of every teacher, even and especially in the earliest grades. In fact, the focus on knowledge development may be one of the most dramatic recent, standards-based curricular shifts for literacy instruction; in the early grades in particular it builds an instructional emphasis on understanding text content (Cervetti & Hiebert, 2015). This emphasis goes beyond generic strategy instruction to teaching students to identify text structures, main ideas, and details; cite evidence; and compare across texts. Of course, essential skills such as concepts about print, decoding, and comprehension strategies cannot be neglected. Comprehension, or message getting from a variety of text types, however, remains the essential goal of reading:

> Comprehension is not an aspect of thinking that emerges only after children have done the reading or passed through the first two years of school. All educators need to hold as their top priority the expectation that learners will understand what they are reading . . . learners should know that all literacy acts involve comprehension. (Clay, 2014, p. 231)

Informational texts provide an excellent means for achieving this goal.

Children's knowledge building requires more than an accumulation of facts about a topic or topics. Instead, it is focused on development of children's knowledge networks and clusters of concepts around a topic (Neuman, Kaefer, & Pinkhorn, 2014). Literacy experiences that encourage this understanding of deep content knowledge move children beyond fact seeking to concept development.

Why Does Knowledge Matter?

Knowledge is integral to literacy development and supports numerous aspects of children's literacy learning:

- ***Reading Proficiency.*** Readers who know more about a text's topic make fewer oral reading and meaning-based errors (Priebe, Keenan, & Miller, 2012). When students have knowledge about a topic, they take in text features more quickly, freeing up their attention for a focus on text meaning (Hirsch, 2003).

- *Academic Vocabulary.* Knowledge of text topics facilitates readers' understanding of different word combinations and selection of appropriate meanings for words (Hirsch, 2003).
- *Comprehension.* Topical knowledge supports comprehension for readers of all ages and all abilities in reading both expository and narrative texts (see Pearson, Hansen, & Gordon, 1979). Furthermore, students with domain knowledge, or deep knowledge about a particular topic, are better able to make inferences about big ideas in a text rather than simply recall facts (Taft & Leslie, 1985), make connections across portions of a text (Rapp, van den Broek, McMaster, Kendeou, & Espin, 2007), and persist in working out meanings in ambiguous texts (McNamara & Kintsch, 1996).

Background knowledge can also support children with emergent reading skills. Strong background knowledge may help children "fill in the blanks" while reading complex texts that challenge their current reading skills (Miller & Keenan, 2009). Content knowledge can thus provide some foundational support while young readers continue to expand their knowledge of print concepts, letters and words, and comprehension strategies. Such strengths, then, allow children to use early literacy processing strategies for monitoring, searching for information, and self-correction (Clay, 2001, 2014). All too often, however, children who do not engage in frequent reading lack the topical knowledge so essential to reading success.

Students need knowledge to understand the academic languages of disciplines like mathematics, history, art, music, and science. Furthermore, they need the ability to think like mathematicians, historians, artists, musicians, or scientists while comprehending or constructing text. The need to not only understand but also evaluate information is crucial in today's world (Moss, 2005). Standards call for children to learn how to evaluate arguments and evidence, and interpret information and draw conclusions (e.g., Partnership for 21st Century Skills, 2013). This learning, however, requires a rich, rigorous curriculum grounded in disciplinary content in science, art, music, social studies, and mathematics. Exposure to the content of informational texts is central to this curriculum.

Building Children's Knowledge with Texts

Knowledge *building* is not the same as the knowledge *activation* teachers commonly do prior to having students read a text. Many teachers do extensive prereading preparation with children, sometimes at the expense of actual reading time. For example, prior to having 2nd-grade children read a text describing how zoos are run or how animal habitats at the zoo are designed and maintained, a teacher might ask students to describe their families' visits to a zoo. This instruction often degenerates into multiple accounts of zoo visits, shifting the focus of the lesson away from the particular topic and information within the text itself and the knowledge students can gain from it.

Building children's deep and wide knowledge does not happen by accident. Teachers must deliberately and intentionally create literacy-learning opportunities focused on expanding children's content knowledge. Effective teachers balance activities designed to activate and build knowledge with teaching designed to show students how to derive that knowledge from text content through their own reading.

> To write, think or solve problems, young learners must have something to write about, something to think about, or some problems to solve. In short, important learning processes require content knowledge. (Neuman, 2001, p. 473)

Because English language arts instruction takes up much of the school day at the earliest grades, integrating science or social studies content with literacy learning is both an effective and efficient means for building disciplinary knowledge.

Creating classroom experiences where students dig deeply into a topic through text sets on a single theme builds webs of knowledge and clusters of concepts. These text sets should represent a range of informational text types. For example, 2nd-grade students studying animal adaptations in science might read a section from their science book as part of a guided reading lesson, engage in a close reading based on a teacher read-aloud of a *Ranger Rick* article about woodpecker adaptations, and complete a shared reading of a trade book like Nicola Davies's (2009) *Extreme Animals: The Toughest Creatures on Earth.* These represent three very different kinds of informational texts. The textbook excerpt is written in an expository style, with a clear focus on conveying facts. The article from *Ranger Rick* is more conversational, whereas the trade book is literary nonfiction and uses narrative devices to create a funny, engaging text accompanied by cartoon illustration. Children can compare and contrast the information, formats, and styles of these three books, to help them understand that all informational texts are not the same. This expanded knowledge base also equips students to comprehend and learn from similar texts they encounter in the future (Duke, Pearson, Strachan, & Billman, 2011).

GAINING KNOWLEDGE THROUGH UNITS OF STUDY

Units of study provide rich opportunities for knowledge building. Many schools and districts have opted to create units of study in response to national and state standards. Such units should

- contribute to the development of foundational reading skills,
- balance literary and informational texts, and include complex texts that let students build knowledge through deep engagement in text,
- focus on academic vocabulary,
- teach strategies that support text comprehension and knowledge building,
- provide varied and substantive writing opportunities, and
- include assessment opportunities that measure progress.

For many teachers, basal readers provide a comfortable framework or structure for reading instruction. By using a basal reader, the teacher is not required to develop materials from "scratch"; many materials are already provided. Units of study, conversely, require teachers to identify pertinent standards; design objectives; read, evaluate, and select materials; develop and sequence activities; and create assessments. Teacher-created units of study allow students to delve deeply into content in ways that basal reader units seldom permit. Recognizing that many teachers are required to use basal readers, however, it is well to remember that the materials in these programs can often be incorporated into larger units of study when suggested resources, instruction, and tasks are chosen and sequenced flexibly and in response to the teacher's instructional goals. In the sections below, we provide guidelines and examples for creating high-quality units of study.

Units of Study: A Rationale

Units of study provide an opportunity for in-depth study of particular topics (different people, times, places, and phenomena) and link interdisciplinary content and contextual academic vocabulary within a topic. Units of study also streamline content delivery. By addressing multiple standards, objectives, and content areas within a broad theme, teachers can craft rich, meaningful instructional tasks that address multiple standards at once. Units of study teach children about the nature of informational texts both individually and in comparison to one another. In-depth text comparisons let children see commonalities and differences in books in terms of theme, structure, style, and concepts, and support children's development of analytic and critical thinking. Finally, thematic units positively influence children's reading and writing development and academic achievement. Through meaningful engagement in reading, writing, speaking, and listening, children grow as literacy learners.

Despite these potential benefits, some cautions are in order. Successful units of study are challenging to create and require extensive planning prior to and during implementation.

Planning Units of Study

The flowchart in Figure 4.1 outlines the key areas of unit development described in the following sections.

Teachers should work in grade-level teams when planning units of study. This collaborative effort makes the workload lighter and helps teachers share their best ideas. Planning considerations include selecting themes, scope, and essential questions; choosing standards and objectives; selecting materials; and creating high-quality tasks, activities, and unit assessments.

Selecting Unit Themes, Scope, and Essential Questions

Units should have a clear focus, last no longer than 3 or 4 weeks, and be conceptually rich, relevant to children's lives, and able to lend themselves to multiple resources. Topics like Water or Our World are likely to be too broad, for example, whereas a unit on Dental Health is too restrictive. In contrast, broadening the topic Dental Health into a unit exploring the human body or nutrition creates more possibilities for in-depth learning.

Choosing a theme that can be conceptually based is another key consideration. Although many primary teachers develop units on topics such as pumpkins, these units are often not conceptually based and thus are too narrow to promote critical thinking. Using broader concepts like Animal Adaptations, contrasting concepts such as City or Country, or controversial topics like "Should we have zoos?" creates stronger potential for greater depth of knowledge and critical thinking.

Essential questions provide a unifying focus for conceptually based units of study. These are broad in scope, open, universal by nature, and able to elicit multiple responses from children. They stimulate thinking, demand evidence, and can be asked and answered at multiple points during a unit. A sample listing of themes, content areas, and essential questions suitable for K–2 units of study is shown in Figure 4.2.

Standards and objectives serve as signposts for student learning and are crucial elements of teachers' planning. Strong thematic units of study, for example, address multiple standards. These may include such standards as the CCSS or *Next Generation Science Standards*. Objectives keep teachers

Figure 4.1. Planning a Unit of Study

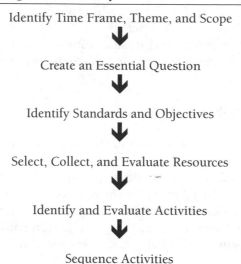

Identify Time Frame, Theme, and Scope

⬇

Create an Essential Question

⬇

Identify Standards and Objectives

⬇

Select, Collect, and Evaluate Resources

⬇

Identify and Evaluate Activities

⬇

Sequence Activities

⬇

Balance Activities

⬇

Identify Formative and Summative Assessments

Figure 4.2. Content Areas, Themes, and Essential Questions

Content Area	Themes	Essential Questions
Social Studies	Communities	What is a community?
Science	Nutrition	What should we eat?
Science	Habitats	What makes a good home?
Social Studies	Alike and Different	What does it mean to be alike and different?
Procedural Texts	English Language Arts	What can procedural texts teach us?

and students focused on specific key goals for learning that drive instruction and provide the basis for assessment.

Selecting Materials

Children's trade books, textbooks, magazines, pamphlets, primary source materials, newspapers, and digital resources such as online videos, magazines, podcasts, websites, webcams, and webinars all enhance children's understanding of particular themes. As teachers explore materials, they need to consider age appropriateness, quality, relevance to the unit, and interest for students.

Resources should also be considered in relationship to one another. Are they representative of multiple genres? Are there clear areas of comparison and contrast among them? Will they provide rich opportunities for discussion? Do they depict diversity in terms of cultural groups and viewpoints?

Creating High-Quality Tasks and Activities

A unit of study is no better than the quality of its activities and student tasks. Student involvement enhances children's cognitive engagement with important ideas, rather than simply time on task (Brophy & Alleman, 1991). An activity is effective when it sparks children's active thinking about content and improves their ability to apply content to real-world questions.

Reading and Writing Activities. Unit reading activities include read-alouds, shared reading, guided reading, independent reading, and close reading. Read-aloud titles introduce and extend units of study and extend student thinking. Guided reading titles should be at students' instructional levels (with appropriate amount and types of challenge), and promote strategic reading of content information. Close reading, too, promotes these goals, particularly for complex texts. Finally, independent reading books should reflect a variety of student interests within a particular theme, be appropriate for a range of readers, and allow for children's choice of reading material.

Writing. Activities to engage children in text construction can include the following:

- Dialogue journals record written conversations between individuals. Children may elect to dialogue with one another or with the teacher.
- Learning logs provide a record of information children gain as they progress through a particular unit.
- Language Experience Approach (Stauffer, 1970) involves having an adult record children's dictation about unit learning. For example, a child might dictate a "fact book" about how a seed grows. Children typically read and reread these dictated texts, and learn how to read and write a small set of interesting words from within the text.
- Children may write and/or illustrate individual reports or class books. By writing their own informational books on topics of

interest, students learn about the features and structures of this genre. "How-to" books about completing a task, or "All About" books that provide facts about an animal, sport, or other interests motivate both reading and writing.

Speaking and Listening. Children should talk about texts at every opportunity. This is important for all children, but especially so for English learners and struggling readers. Speaking and listening activities include the following:

- Children can engage in a wide variety of dramatic activities, including spontaneous role-playing, creative movement, pantomime, interpretive drama, puppetry, and Readers Theatre (Sloyer, 1982).
- Oral retellings deepen children's comprehension of complex informational text. They can facilitate information recall, enhance academic vocabulary, and sensitize students to text structures. The use of flannel boards or other props enhances this experience.
- Choral readings involve children in reading poems, stories, or songs with lyrical language related to unit themes.

Literacy activities that incorporate drawing, painting, sculpture, collages, and murals are just a few of the many possible ways in which art may be used to extend the literary experience. Likewise, music can provide another creative means for enhancing literary experiences. Children can learn songs, compose their own songs, create musical scores, develop performances, or set poems to music.

Sequencing and Balancing Activities

Sequencing of unit activities typically involves (1) creating initiating activities to kick off and build interest in a unit; (2) engagement activities that involve reading, writing, speaking, and listening; and (3) culminating activities, typically involving an assessment in the form of a project or writing activity. Initiating activities create excitement for the unit and include a read-aloud, fieldtrip, video, or movie. Engagement activities create opportunities for large- and small-group reading, writing, speaking, and listening experiences as described earlier. Culminating activities help students summarize and extend unit learning and are designed to measure how well children have met unit objectives.

Teachers must balance reading, writing, speaking, and listening; hands-on versus pencil-and-paper activities; and those requiring students to work independently or with teacher support. Large-group, small-group, paired, and individual activities must also be balanced. Figure 4.3 presents questions teachers can use to consider the quality of unit resources and activities they create.

Unit Assessment

Assessment is used to determine whether the objectives of the unit have been met. Unit evaluation should be both formative and summative—that is, it should provide for ongoing assessment as well as overall evaluation of the unit.

Formative assessments should be ongoing and include a variety of ways to check for understanding. For example, learning logs, dialogue journals, and even dramatizations as described earlier can all be forms of formative assessment. Teacher checklists, anecdotal records, and students' daily work samples also help teachers assess student progress. Summative assessments that involve performance tasks like formal writing assignments, projects, and reports provide a rich record of unit learning. These "far transfer" assessments are those that engage students in application of those skills targeted by the unit of study within a new and different context (Pearson, Valencia, & Wixson, 2014). These assessments measure students' robust learning: their ability to integrate their learning with new knowledge or solve problems they have not yet examined. Examining student progress using a wide variety of assessments gives the teacher and the student a more valid picture of gains in ability and progress toward goals.

A Sample Unit of Study

Alice, a 1st-grade teacher, created a conceptually rich unit of study on habitats that effectively integrates science and literacy. Figure 4.4 provides a listing of resources used for this unit of study.

In the following section, Alice thinks aloud about her planning:

My unit on Habitats was created with our 1st-grade teachers. It has a science focus, and students learn about science through reading, writing, speaking, and listening. We crafted an essential question that our 1st-graders can connect to and build upon: What makes a good home?

My unit incorporates a standard from the *Next Generation Science Standards* that asks students to design a solution to a human problem. This task also forms the basis for the unit's summative assessment. In addition, I've integrated many CCSS related to informational text comprehension and writing. My objectives extend logically from

Figure 4.3. Evaluating Unit Resources and Activities

Individual Resources. Is the resource . . .	Checklist
Appropriate to the theme of the unit of study?	
Related to the unit focus and objectives?	
Appropriate to students' age, reading levels, and conceptual levels?	
Conducive to teaching foundational skills and strategic comprehension?	
Conceptually rich?	
Multiple Resources	
Do materials represent different genre?	
Do they contribute to knowledge building and reinforce academic vocabulary development across sources?	
Are there areas of comparison and contrast between resources?	
Do materials reflect different points of view about a problem or issue?	
Will materials prompt rich discussions and reflective inquiry?	
Evaluating Activities. Are activities . . .	
Feasible in terms of time, resources, space, and equipment?	
Of appropriate difficulty?	
Interesting and engaging for all students?	
Rich with cognitive engagement potential?	
Balancing Activities. Is there balance between . . .	
Reading, writing, and speaking and listening activities?	
Hands-on versus paper-and-pencil tasks?	
Independent versus teacher-directed activities?	
Large-group, small-group, paired, and individual activities?	

these standards and focus on higher-level thinking, going beyond identification and explanation. The summative assessment, too, is clearly aligned with my standards and objectives. It addresses both the problem of endangered animals and literacy standards for reading and writing informational texts. I will address academic vocabulary by focusing attention on 13 key terms crucial to the topic of habitats. We will keep vocabulary notebooks, create word walls, and do vocabulary sorting to provide daily attention to these terms.

I found lots of great online resources for the unit, including habitat-related texts from Engage NY and webcams from the Monterey museum (see Figure 4.4) that let my students see animals in their habitats worldwide. I've picked lots of books about animals and habitats for students to compare. I'm also excited to use *I See a Kookaburra: Animal Habitats Around the World* (Jenkins, 2005) to introduce the unit. I also found some great leveled informational texts for guided reading groups from National Geographic and Crabtree Publishing.

Selected lesson activities are described in the next section to provide an overview of children's multidimensional engagement during the lesson.

Implementing the Unit. To begin the unit, Alice will read aloud *I See a Kookaburra: Animal Habitats Around the World* to pique student interest in the topic. As she reads about each animal and its habitat, she will record information on an illustrated interactive chart to provide a focal point for the entire unit. Students will refer to, add, and classify animal pictures and names according to habitats as the unit progresses.

Engagement Activities. Children will engage in reading, writing, speaking, and listening activities in large and small groups. They will learn about individual animals and their habitats, compare and contrast animals and habitats, and then focus on endangered species and their habitats.

Whole-Group Lessons:
- Organizing shared reading of selected titles related to the topic
- Watching online webcams within different environments; discussing and recording observations in learning logs through pictures and/or print
- Completing vocabulary notebooks and sorting terms on the word wall to work with academic vocabulary
- Teaching a close reading lesson during a read-aloud of *Starfish* (Hurd, 2000)
- Performing a Readers Theatre about endangered animals
- Using demonstration lessons about online searching to prepare students for information gathering for the culminating inquiry research poster

Small-Group Lessons:
- Organizing guided reading using leveled books to address essential standards such as asking and answering questions and identifying main ideas and key details, as well as foundational skills and vocabulary development

Figure 4.4. Resources

Print Material:

- *Almost Gone! The World's Rarest Animals*, Jenkins, 2006, Harper-Collins.
- *Amazing Whales!*, Thomson, 2006, HarperCollins.
- *Animal Habitats,* National Geographic Windows on Literacy Language, Literacy and Vocabulary.
- *Introducing Habitats* series, Crabtree Publishing.
- *I See a Kookaburra: Animal Habitats Around the World*, Jenkins, 2005, Houghton Mifflin Harcourt.
- *Polar Bears, What Lives in a Tide Pool, The Rain Forest,* National Geographic Windows on Literacy Early (Science: Life Science).
- *Starfish* (Let's Read and Find Out), Hurd, 2000, HarperCollins.

Online Material:

- Earth's Endangered Creatures: http://earthsendangered.com/index-_s.asp
- Engage NY Domain 8: Animals and Habitats: https://www.engageny.org/resource/grade-1-ela-domain-8-animals-and-habitats
- Engage NY Domain 8: Downloadable resources: https://www.engageny.org/sites/default/files/downloadable-resources/ckla_g1_d8_anth.pdf
- Kids' Planet, Defenders of Wildlife: www.kidsplanet.org
- Monterey Bay Aquarium Live Web Cams: www.montereybayaquarium.org/animals-and-experiences/live-web-cams
- National Geographic Kids: http://kids.nationalgeographic.com/kids/
- National Geographic, Starfish: http://animals.nationalgeographic.com/animals/invertebrates/starfish/
- National Wildlife Foundation, Florida Panther: https://www.nwf.org/Wildlife/Wildlife-Library/Mammals/Florida-Panther.aspx
- World Wildlife Fund-Florida Panther: https://www.nwf.org/Wildlife/Wildlife-Library/Mammals/Florida-Panther.aspx

---

- Retelling selected titles (*Polar Bears* and *The Rain Forest*) to partners at children's tables
- Reading the Readers Theatre script on endangered animals with a fluency partner

Culminating Activities:
- Pairing students to perform online research on a selected endangered animal and its habitat supported by graphic organizers
- Pairing students to create posters that include information on an endangered animal, its appearance, its habitat, threats to its survival, and two ways it might be saved

Grade-Appropriate Collaborative Research

At the end of the Habitats unit, Alice felt that her students were ready for a challenging summative assessment. The inquiry research project poster required children to synthesize their learning about animals and their habitats, apply this knowledge to assess humans' impact on habitat, and identify two ways the animal might be saved from extinction. Because most of her 1st-graders had not engaged in research before, Alice planned to carefully scaffold each step in the process. Because this project required students to gather, synthesize, and organize information, it represented an important precursor to the report writing that would happen later in the year. Alice began the project this way:

> *Alice:* Good morning, students. Today we are going to begin our poster projects on endangered animals. Let's review what the word *endangered* means. Do you see a root word inside this word?
> *Alex:* Yes, it is *danger*.
> *Alice:* So what do you think *endangered* means?
> *Maria:* It is an animal in danger or in trouble.
> *Alice:* Yes. And why are some animals in danger?

The children worked with a partner to think, pair, and share, and identified ways that humans are harming the habitats of animals, including the killing of animals, the introduction of chemicals, and pollution. Alice then read *Almost Gone: The World's Rarest Animals* (Jenkins, 2006) aloud to remind children of animals they might use for their reports and add to the list of reasons animal habitats are threatened.

> *Preparing Students for the Research Process.* Alice presented students with a list of endangered animals they could use for their poster. She paired students strategically by placing a stronger reader with an emergent reader to ensure success. Each pair identified an animal they wanted to study. Alice explained to students that they would be reading books and online sources in order to find information about their animals. She provided students with a graphic organizer that identified the key areas about which they would collect information: What does my

animal look like? What is its habitat? Why is it endangered? And how can it be protected? Alice also introduced resources to her students: "To find the information you need for your poster, you can use books or the computer. I have selected books from the library that can help you, and I have bookmarked websites on the computer related to many of the animals. Try to use two sources, a book and a website, to find your information." Alice had carefully selected resources at a range of reading levels. For those students who were not yet reading, she bookmarked websites that read information aloud, as well online videos and webcams of as many of the animals as she could find.

Modeling How to Locate Information. Alice knew that students would need help locating information from these sources and completing their graphic organizers. She had previously taught them how to find information from a book using the table of contents, headings, and indices, but Alice knew that her students needed support in using online sources. She presented a website titled *Florida Panther* from the National Wildlife Foundation website (see Figure 4.4). Although it was challenging, headings were clearly identified. She thought aloud as she showed students how they might extract information to record on their graphic organizers in answer to the first question above:

> Before I look at this website, I want to review the information I am looking for. My graphic organizer asks that I answer these questions: *How does my animal look? Where does it live? Why is it endangered? How can it be protected?* I might find the answers to the first three questions, but I will need to figure out the answer to the last question myself. Let's look at this website about the Florida panther that I found online. It does have bolded headings that I can skim and scan to find what I need.
>
> To answer my first question I will see if I can find any words about what it looks like. One of the bolded words is description. That section will tell me what a Florida panther looks like. The first sentence says, "They are large tan cats." Later in the section it says they have black on their ears and tails. I don't need to write down all these words. I will pick the VIP words—the very important words. I think *large tan cats* and *black tails and ears* are the important words, so I will write them on my organizer. I also see the bolded word *size*; it says panthers are six to seven feet long. I'll add that too.

At this point, students worked in pairs to gather information from the books and the bookmarked websites. They completed the first three questions on their graphic organizers. This took several days and required additional small-group scaffolding for some students. Students also completed posters in pairs. After they completed these, each pair presented what they had learned to the entire class. Following this, students presented their posters at parent night, which allowed them to share their learning with a wider audience.

SUMMARY

Informational texts are an essential component of classroom literacy instruction. Early exposure to these texts ensures that children experience the knowledge building so essential for 21st-century literacy needs. To ensure that students are given the knowledge-building opportunities required for academic success, teachers should begin by enacting the following recommendations:

- Integrate literacy instruction with disciplinary instruction in science, social science, mathematics, art, and music.
- Increase the use of informational text in the classroom, and engage students in reading a wide range of informational texts on related themes.
- Create a thematic unit that incorporates at least one other discipline and engages students in reading, writing, speaking, and listening.
- Engage students in an online research project.

Units of study represent a rich opportunity for students to engage in deep study of a conceptually rich topic. Creating units of study requires that teachers identify high-quality themes, essential questions, standards and objectives, a range of materials, and a variety of activities involving reading, writing, speaking, and listening in pursuit of disciplinary knowledge.

Close reading of informational texts represents another way that teachers can build student knowledge. By using complex texts that stretch students through engagement with literal, inferential, application, and text dependent questions, teachers continue to build disciplinary knowledge through the study of academic language and text structure.

Collaborative research activities teach children to be knowledge seekers, locating, analyzing, and synthesizing information in books or online resources. Through these experiences, children learn to sift through information, identify key ideas, develop inferencing skills, and share information with peers and others.

Further Reading

Clay, M. M. (2014). Constructive processes: Reading, writing, talking, art and crafts. In *By different paths to common outcomes*: *Literacy learning and teaching* (pp. 200–210). Auckland, New Zealand: Global Education Systems.

> In this inspiring chapter, Clay linked developmental learning to classroom activities that encourage children to engage in constructive processes—using what they know to create murals, poetry, pottery, storytelling, dramatic plays, and paintings. Clay articulated her own advocacy of the crucial role of arts and crafts in learning within this chapter, including an insightful explanation of how such activities expand children's thinking and help teachers understand how well children have learned how to use knowledge constructively.

Lapp, D., Moss, B., Grant, M., & Johnson, K. (2015). *A close look at close reading: Teaching students to analyze complex texts. Grades K–5.* Alexandria, VA: Association for Supervision and Curriculum Development.

> This book provides teachers with in-depth information on how to scaffold close readings for all students. It details how to evaluate texts for complexity, how to create scaffolded lessons based on teaching points derived from this analysis, and how to differentiate instruction in ways that facilitate learning. This text also contains chapters that address the ways that oral language development, writing, and assessment are integral to the close reading processes.

CHAPTER 5

Learning to Write Informational Text

Learning how to write is an essential accomplishment for young children. Communicating, recording, and entertaining readers through written language is a highly rewarding literacy activity. Writing also supports children's overall literacy processing; children's engagement in both reading and writing creates common stores of knowledge about foundational skills. Reading and writing require similar processes as children search for information, solve words, or organize information effectively (Clay, 2001).

This chapter illustrates the characteristics of effective writing instruction to ensure that children become writers as well as readers. The following focus questions will be useful to consider while reading this chapter:

1. What kinds of cognitive processing do children use during writing?
2. How can teachers ensure that the needs of diverse students (including English language learners) for writing are addressed?
3. How can young writers focus their attention on spelling while writing without losing sight of their intended messages?
4. What is the role of drafting in young children's writing development?
5. What instructional support do children need during independent writing?
6. How can sufficient writing instruction fit into a daily classroom schedule?

WRITING AS ACTIVE PROBLEM SOLVING

This chapter is organized around Matt's experiences during two 1st-grade writing lessons. In October of his 1st-grade year, Matt was experiencing significant difficulties in literacy learning. He was a friendly and engaged student, however, and demonstrated strong interests in both narrative stories and informational texts. The first writing lesson, as observed by this book's first author and described below, was not effective for Matt and other students. The second lesson, however, included improved instructional techniques that met Matt's writing needs much more successfully. The sections below describe crucial differences between the two writing lessons and relate these differences to Clay's observations of children's writing development. Young children must learn how to utilize their own knowledge and experiences when writing, compose ideas into written language, understand how to use letters and words to represent information, take risks in their writing, and reread to monitor and self-correct (Clay, 2001, 2014). Children, then, use a multidimensional set of complex behaviors when writing. Accordingly, we present an explanation in this chapter of best teaching practices based on Clay's research, theories, and recommendations for practice.

Matt's Initial Writing Lesson

Matt's teacher, Grace, had become concerned over her students' limited progress in writing skills. Grace was an experienced, successful, and dedicated 1st-grade teacher working with children with a wide range of academic achievement, language, and ethnicity. Her concerns grew out of her own ongoing evaluation of students' writing products. Consequently, Grace (in collaboration with the other 1st-grade teachers at her school) set a goal to improve her writing instruction. Grace and her 1st-grade colleagues invited this book's first author to observe lessons and provide coaching to assist with needed shifts in instruction. This group of teachers were already working diligently to address the needs of students by implementing important aspects of effective writing instruction. The teachers had studied the use of graphic organizers in classroom lessons, for example, to teach the structure of informational text to students. They had also incorporated direct prompting for writing strategies into lessons ("Before you start writing, always think of your sentence first" and "Now I'm going to go back and reread what I wrote, to see if it makes sense"). In spite of these positive steps, Grace and her colleagues were not yet convinced that their instruction was the best help for their students. The sections below describe our collaborative search to match writing instruction to children's needs.

Grace taught an initial, whole-class lesson focused on writing an informational report (observed by our first author). Grace informed her students that they would be writing three sentences about sheep based on their recent read-aloud sessions on that same topic. Grace began with an explicit demonstration using a three-column chart (see Figure 5.1) to help students organize information before writing.

Grace filled in several examples on this chart, using children's suggestions to state what a sheep *has*, *can do*, and *is*. Grace then showed her

Figure 5.1. Grace's 3-Column Chart

A sheep . . .

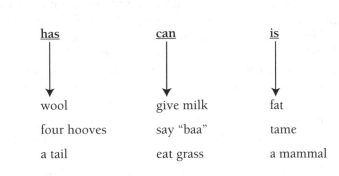

has	can	is
wool	give milk	fat
four hooves	say "baa"	tame
a tail	eat grass	a mammal

students how to write a first sentence from the chart. As she wrote *A sheep has a tail*, she explained how she referred back to the chart for sentence structure: "If I look here, then I'll know what to write first: *A sheep has*. Then I can choose *a tail* for my first sentence." Grace used think-aloud to demonstrate her use of a spelling strategy: "Okay, I'll say *sheep* slowly. The sounds I hear will help me know what letters to write." Grace finished by reminding her students that their own three sentences needed to be finished before recess time. Grace's students were given 10 minutes for independent writing. She expected them to write individually and independently during this time, as this would be required for district-mandated benchmark assessments.

Grace had, of course, incorporated several kinds of strong instructional support in her lesson: a graphic organizer, an explicit writing demonstration, and an explanation of several important writing strategies. Grace, however, was not convinced that the lesson had actually improved her students' writing skills. This impression was confirmed as Grace, her colleagues, and our first author met and evaluated what students had written during the lesson. The 1st-grade team together identified a wide range of student writing. Strong, average, and poor writers in the room, however, utilized writing behaviors that were very similar to those used in previous activities and demonstrated little evidence of progress.

Together, the 1st-grade team and coach identified the following concerns. In spite of obvious interest in the read-aloud discussions about the lives of sheep, children were only minimally engaged during writing. Stronger writers in the room completed the three required sentences within 2 to 3 minutes (and spent the rest of the time talking quietly to a neighbor). We found no evidence in students' written texts or writing behavior that they had engaged in new exploration or extended learning; Grace's strong writers were not observed to use overt writing strategies, text revision, or collaboration with other writers.

Grace's average writers copied from the board to complete three sentences. They occasionally articulated sounds in an unknown word to approximate a phonetic spelling. Although Grace did circulate as students wrote, her interaction with students was primarily to check and confirm that they had completed the task. The coach did not observe interaction focused on extending children's writing skill. Even as children completed the basic writing task with time to spare, for example, Grace had not asked children to elaborate on ideas or construct more complex sentence structures. The 1st-grade team agreed that the structured, three-sentence writing task had, in spite of careful planning, required little thinking or decision-making for most students.

As Matt began to write his own text, he first copied his teacher's sentence from the board: *A sheep has a tail.* Matt, like other poor writers in the room, was not able to accomplish much beyond this copying task. He started on his second sentence and wrote the word *A* independently. Next, however, Matt made many attempts to spell the word *sheep*, erasing each one and starting again. He used all the remaining writing time (about 7 minutes) for these unsuccessful attempts and his paper developed a ragged hole where he had erased repeatedly. Just as the class began to gather for morning recess, the child sitting next to Matt leaned over and whispered, "*Sheep* is up there [pointing to the board]." Matt copied the word and went to recess.

Both the teachers' analysis of students' writing products and the coach's observation of children's real-time writing behavior, then, provided little evidence of student learning. Together, the teachers and coach explored possible causes for this lack of progress. Grace noted, insightfully, that her students did more or less exactly what she had asked of them. Grace had supplied a step-by-step explanation and demonstration of a narrowly defined, routine task to the whole class and did not provide extended support for children as they were writing. All students' writing was simple and straightforward, and most of the 10-minute time frame was spent copying from the teacher's first sentence and chart.

Matt's learning was also of grave concern to both teachers and the coach. He did not, for example, construct a draft that communicated his own ideas and interests. He would not have been able to share this writing usefully with an audience or engage in revision during future writing activities. During this lesson, Matt had simply copied his teacher's sentence and engaged in an ineffective struggle to spell a challenging word. Although Matt remained at work during this independent writing time, he did not engage as a writer. Writing must be understood as a constructive activity, requiring children's active engagement in composing and communicating ideas while at the same time managing letter writing, spelling, and concepts about print (Clay, 2014). This first writing lesson did not provide Matt with the opportunity he needed to practice written communication of ideas using a set of complex and comprehensive processing strategies.

This first writing lesson might be described as an "explain and test" model: provide information in a graphic organizer and require students to write independently to a narrow formula with little or no support. Instruction, however, should not be implemented in ways that oversimplify complex tasks and thus inadvertently "protect" children from the need to engage in their own thinking and use of strategic activity. Grace had provided initial support to her students through her presentation of an organizing chart and key language for constructing informational text. The teachers and coach both agreed, however, that children's responses to this lesson demonstrated a need for additional in-the-moment instructional support and collaboration with peers. Grace's students needed shifts in instruction with opportunities to learn how to

- attend closely to the features of letters,
- construct words using phonemes and spelling patterns,
- direct attention to serial order and spaces between words,
- break down the writing task into letters and words, and
- simultaneously construct sentences and convey information. (Clay, 2001, p. 15)

Together, the 1st-grade team and coach considered several ways to enhance future writing instruction for stronger student engagement and success. The description, below, of Grace's subsequent lesson illustrates both the resulting shifts that were incorporated into Grace's teaching and her students' responses. We also connect principles of effective writing instruction to key aspects of this subsequent lesson. These principles include learning and using writing strategies; expanding children's knowledge, thinking, and language; using systematic observation to incorporate differentiated instruction into writing lessons; and allowing sufficient classroom time for writing instruction and practice.

A Second, Improved Writing Lesson

The instructional activities that Grace implemented in a subsequent lesson acknowledged that children's learning does not depend entirely on close adherence to the structure of a teacher-provided demonstration. She began by telling her students that they were going to create their own notes, using both words and pictures. As she read a brief excerpt aloud from an informational book on foxes, Grace stopped every few sentences and asked students to decide what facts had been presented. Grace then gave students a few minutes to make a quick drawing at their seats: "Your drawing will help you to remember what was most interesting to you about this information and then you can use it in your own writing." Students started with a quick line drawing of a fox. As the discussion continued, they each added at least one fact that was of interest. Examples included labeling of the fox as a mammal or the fox's bushy tail with the phrase "keeps it warm." As Grace asked the class to decide on a final fact that they liked the most, students enthusiastically noted facts such as a fox's nose helps it smell prey. Grace asked them to draw and write a last note together with their neighbor: "Make a good picture and label to help you remember what you're most interested in."

Writing Couplets. The verbal and visual notes that Grace's students created provided ready access to organized information. Even so, Grace's students were not yet ready to write. They needed active rehearsal to support their use of the more sophisticated language structures of informational text. From her analysis of recent writing samples, Grace decided that writing in couplets (Donovan & Smolkin, 2011) would be a good next step for her students. Couplets combine two related clauses for a statement and reason, or a statement with examples. Grace had students repeat an example orally with emphasis on the connecting word *because*: "A fox has a bushy tail because it keeps it warm." She then asked students to use their own verbal and visual notes and orally rehearse similar couplets with a neighbor.

Finally, Grace reminded students to use their notes and work with their partners to write their story about foxes. She briefly posted and read a chart showing what they should do if they got stuck while writing (see Figure 5.2).

In a subsequent discussion, the 1st-grade team and coach agreed that this second lesson had sparked children's interests and allowed them further scope as writers. Every writer was observed to stretch his or her own learning: writing more text overall, using the more complicated couplet structure, and incorporating his or her own items of interest into the writing.

Figure 5.2. Grace's Strategy Chart

If you get stuck . . .

- Read a book about your ideas
- Reread your writing
- Check your notes
- Talk to a friend
- Ask for help

Matt did not simply copy a teacher-demonstrated sentence in this lesson. Instead, he referred back to his own verbal and visual notes and conferred with his partner: "Its ears are so pointy. I like that one!" When Matt came to the difficult-to-spell word *pointy*, he asked his partner for assistance. She articulated the sounds within the word, and Matt wrote *pointy* as *pte*. This approximated spelling allowed Matt to put phonemic awareness into practice, demonstrating for himself that a slow articulation of sounds within a word is a useful spelling strategy that could allow him to write with more independence. Matt completed a four-sentence text in 10 minutes—a text that was both of interest to Matt and that could serve as a useful starting point for future sharing and revision activities. Matt, then, had engaged as a writer.

The following sections illustrate the significance of the changes Grace made in her writing instruction, arising from her collaborative inquiry with colleagues and the coach and in connection to Clay's literacy processing theory. Specific suggestions for differentiated teaching are highlighted, beginning with the need for explicit instruction combined with teacher guidance while children write.

CONSTRUCTING IDEAS INTO WRITTEN LANGUAGE

The acquisition of literacy processing "begins when a child is expected to compose and write a simple message or read a simple continuous text" (Clay, 2001, p. 97). Continuous text is authentic text that conveys information, ideas, and relationships between ideas across sentences and paragraphs. Children's active and successful reading and writing of continuous text is central to processes that build the knowledge of strategies needed for strong literacy learning.

Guided Support While Children Write

Writing requires simultaneous attention to information from a variety of sources. Instruction teaches children how to manage complex decision-making while writing: how to compose a sentence that conveys intended messages clearly, or how to remember to leave a space before writing a new word. Clay (2001) noted that children have to bring together ideas, compose a message, search for ways to record ideas, and monitor the message as it is constructed. An effective context for children's writing includes sufficient teacher and peer collaboration to avoid roadblocks. After drawing, labeling, discussing, and rehearsing information and language structures, for instance, Matt paid brief, momentary attention to a spelling strategy. He did so without losing momentum as a writer; he was able to listen to sounds within the word while still holding on to the ideas and language structures he needed to continue writing. Matt's interaction with peers was both structured and encouraged as he collaborated on his verbal and visual notes and orally rehearsed the language of couplets. These instructional improvements created a more developmentally friendly writing context, and expanded Matt's thinking into more sophisticated thought, language, and strategies while writing.

It is tempting to assume that a lack of immediate guidance for a task will cause children to become more independent. There are no shortcuts to children's proficient performance on benchmark assessments, however. The only way to be sure that children will perform well on writing assessments is to ensure that they learn how to write. Independence occurs as children learn how to initiate and control their own learning (Clay, 1991b; Watson, 1999). It is fostered by instructional decisions that construct and support children's task engagement. Instructional scaffolding teaches children how to write with increasing independence through explanation, modeling, and prompting. Children's independent writing, then, is not a solitary activity. Like independent reading (e.g., Moss & Young, 2010), independent writing is an instructional framework. Teachers should teach during independent writing. They should circulate around the room and prompt children to use strategies, provide a few minutes of instruction to small groups of children, and conduct informal, 1- to 2-minute coaching conferences with individual writers.

Composing has to be learned (Clay, 2001). Translating ideas into written language does not occur automatically simply because the writer has ideas or a topic. Children need practice considering and manipulating ideas and interests into written language, moving from ideas to spoken language structures and finally to printed messages (Clay, 2001). Mimicking the pattern in a storybook, or copying the teacher's writing, does not allow children the opportunities needed to learn how to compose written text with independence (Clay, 2014). Even emergent writers have ideas, interests, and oral language. If given opportunities, children will use what they know about printed language to explore writing—progressing toward conventional writing from scribbling to letter-like forms, writing with a few known letters, and finally writing with known words and spelling strategies. In order to do so, however, children must be engaged in constructing comprehensive knowledge about the integration of language and print (Sulzby, 1992).

Children's time to write is a valuable instructional framework. Occasional teacher prompting ensures that students are not completing easy writing tasks without extending their reach into new territory. A teacher might pause briefly with a student who has written a short but simple text, for example, and say, "How could you introduce your readers to the next part of your description?" Or, for another student who has written *fast* as *fat*, "That's a good start, but say *fast* slowly to yourself and see what sound you missed." It is also useful to work briefly with two or three students at a small table after other children have settled into their own writing. Grace, for example, might call Matt and several other children to her table just as the rest of the class begins to write. She might talk with this group about their notes and ideas, and take a few minutes to get them started writing successfully. Similarly, English language learners would benefit from the opportunity to review and practice what was taught to the whole class in a small group while they begin to write. Children in this type of group, with flexible membership from one day to the next, can work on the very same writing as others in the classroom. The teacher will observe carefully and quietly "lean in" to provide individual assistance and prompting as needed based on specific instructional goals. After getting a small group of children focused on a needed improvement in their writing, Grace can then circulate to assist other students in the classroom.

Learning and Using Writing Strategies

Young writers must learn the "how" of writing: how to carry out problem-solving strategies successfully and independently. Strategic activity is the thinking or action that learners use to pick up information, make decisions, and evaluate the results (Clay, 2005a). A child uses strategic activity, for example, by deciding that the difficult-to-spell word *looks* might be solved by starting with the known word *look*. Figure 5.3 provides a list of prompts teachers use to assist children as they learn to use active problem solving while writing.

Writers consider ideas and topics, make decisions about how to organize those ideas into written language structures, and evaluate the resulting, ongoing draft as it is constructed. Drafting is crucial for children's writing development. Children do not, of course, construct perfectly composed and accurate writing (especially when drafting). They will, however, mostly write drafts, editing and revising only a small percentage of total writing for publication. Even so, children need to use strategic activities on a momentary basis to both write well and gain control over important writing behaviors. Children's strategy use is the mechanism by which they continue to learn about writing (Clay, 2014) and thus create better and better drafts over time. A child's *drafted* writing products, then, should demonstrate gradual, overall improvement over time.

Young writers should spell words, for instance, as best they can with brief attention while still maintaining a focus on intended meanings:

Figure 5.3. Teacher Prompting While Children Write

Category	Teacher Prompting
Directing students' attention to key aspects of composing tasks	Pick one small but interesting idea to write about.
	Think of a title that tells what you are writing about.
	What would be an interesting first sentence for your story?
	How will you introduce your readers to the next part of your story?
	What word(s) would make your readers know what you really mean?
	Could you start the next sentence like this?
Directing students' attention to key aspects of transcribing tasks	Say your sentences. Can you hear where the period/ question mark/exclamation point might go?
	Say that word slowly to yourself. What sounds do you hear?
	Clap that word to help you know what parts to write.
Prompting students to use information from interests and resources	Think about everything you know about this topic.
	Did you read or write something like this that you could look at to help yourself?
Prompting students to monitor their writing as it is being constructed	Say it to yourself before you write it. How should your sentence sound?
	Have you included enough details so that your readers will understand and be interested?
Supporting students' decisions about the next steps to take for writing	What could you do now to help yourself keep writing?
	What information are you thinking about next?
	When you get stuck, rereading will help you to start writing again.
	When you get stuck, talking to yourself or to a friend about your ideas will help you to start writing again.

Source: Gibson, S. A. (2008). An effective framework for primary-grade guided writing lessons. *The Reading Teacher, 62*(4), p. 329. ©2008 International Reading Association. Reprinted with permission from Wiley.

> Spelling occurs during the act of getting the language of ideas and images on a page. It's in the act of drafting when writers need to be able to spell words. After that, they can look up the words, check them electronically, or ask a friend how to spell. Spelling occurs in the draft. (Fearn & Farnan, 2001, p. 404)

Young writers do not need to spell all words correctly. Instead, they need to practice using the strategies they already know for a best attempt that can be completed quickly. Matt's attempt of *pte* for the word *pointy* was good practice given his current knowledge—and thus worthy of praise as is. Another student, however, might be prompted to use a more sophisticated spelling strategy: "Hmm. Clap when you hear the two parts of *pointy*. How do you think *point* might look? Now, what could you add to change *point* into *pointy*?" Learning how to construct new words by using increasingly sophisticated spelling strategies is more valuable than simply attempting to memorize the spelling of every new word (Clay, 2001). Solving the spelling of a new word by analogy with an already known word, for example, is a generative process that directly supports ongoing learning (Clay, 2014). Once a child has learned to use an ending Y for familiar words like *baby* and *candy*, a larger set of similar words becomes easier to spell (*pointy*, *ready*, or *shady*, for example).

Writing is the only authentic context within which young writers can put spelling strategies into practice—gaining experience, feedback on their efforts, and expertise. Teachers should not tell children to simply skip words when writing or that "spelling doesn't count." Matt, for example, clearly felt that his spelling of the word *sheep* "counted." He persevered with multiple, unsuccessful attempts to spell this word correctly. Children demonstrate a strong sense of closure and confidence when a word they are writing is solved to their own satisfaction with or without assistance (using either a best, momentary attempt or conventional spelling). It is the teacher's responsibility to implement instruction, and structure peer collaboration while children write, in ways that allow for successful word solving. Children's use of effective strategic activity for solving words while writing is a necessary element for their engagement as writers.

STUDENT STRENGTHS AND THE CHALLENGES OF INFORMATIONAL TEXT

What children can already do with independence, success, and engagement is the most efficient starting point for new learning. Teachers thus draw on a child's competencies while supporting new and tentative responding (Clay, 2001; Doyle, 2013). Current standards require that children learn how to write informational text with the same types of craftsmanship as has been more typical in their writing of narrative texts (Calkins, Ehrenworth, & Lehman, 2012). Furthermore, 21st-century standards demand writing proficiency as (1) a form of social, literary, and scientific participation across both print and electronic media, and (2) social sharing, to encourage dialogue and to inform and persuade (Yancey, 2009).

Prewriting Processes

Outlining or planning before writing is difficult (and typically unsuccessful) for young writers (e.g., Berninger, Fuller, & Whittaker, 1996). Prewriting activities that include opportunities to choose and dig deeper into interesting topics, draw, rehearse oral-to-written language structures, and collaborate with peers, however, are well matched to children's strengths. It is helpful, then, to conceptualize prewriting instruction as knowledge building and language rehearsal rather than as planning. The CCSS recommend that young writers learn how to research a topic, organize their knowledge, and rehearse the more complex language structures needed for writing (NGACBP & CCSSO, 2010). In our recommended activities children interact with both new knowledge and academic language with increasing depth, preparing them to write effectively.

Building Knowledge. Brainstorming is an effective way to activate and build children's knowledge. Four general procedures are typically used for brainstorming: focusing on quantity, withholding criticism, welcoming unusual ideas, and combining and improving ideas (Osborn, 1953). Children contribute knowledge about the topic from their own experiences while all ideas are recorded without evaluation on a whiteboard or document viewer. Next, children categorize these ideas. In the List Group Label activity (Taba, 1967), children also group related words and phrases together and decide on an explanatory label for each group. They might, for example, list everything they already know about turtles. The teacher would then ask them to decide on items that could be grouped together, and choose a label for each category (food sources, habitat, attributes, etc.). Students are asked to explain why items belong together, giving them an opportunity to articulate their thinking and practice academic language.

Allowing Choice. Choice is an essential ingredient for writers. Choice transforms a closed, constrained writing task into an open-ended one, allowing children to explore and learn from their own writing experiences. Choice, however, requires more than just turning children loose with paper and pencil (Dyson, 1997). Instead, choice should be paired with challenge in order to support children's deeper and more detailed learning.

Closed, constrained tasks (as in the first writing lesson in this chapter) do not provide the rich opportunities children need to appropriate complex uses of language. Clay (2014) specified that all writing activities should be rich enough to provide the opportunities needed to expand competencies. Children may become more practiced with accurate and fluent writing of high-frequency words while synthesizing information into sentences, or using new knowledge to compose an important and clear message, for example. This complex use of language provides opportunities for children to discover new aspects of print (Clay, 2014). It is likely, for example, that a child who decides to write more extensively about various kinds of sheep and how they are cared for on farms will make more mechanical errors than when writing easier, less interesting text. Such errors might include misspellings of words the child has previously spelled correctly, or difficulties with the grammatical structure of more complex sentences. This child will also be much more likely to encounter appropriately challenging new writing tasks—and thus will engage in new learning.

Rehearsal. Language and thought are closely interrelated and language use is a central, underlying expertise needed for all literacy tasks; it is the "operating system" for writers (Fisher, Frey, & Rothenberg, 2008). A writer with ideas and information at hand still must determine how those ideas translate into the sentence, paragraph, and text structures used for written text. Oral rehearsal facilitates each child's fluent flow of ideas for writing, bringing literary forms of language to their ears and tongues—ready for use. This rehearsal entails children's authentic talk and conversation far beyond what is possible in a typical whole-class discussion where one or two children may be called to contribute. Instead, children participate regularly in peer-to-peer collaboration and frequent interaction with the teacher in small groups or brief individual conversations.

In contrast, more traditional teacher-directed prewriting instruction can interfere with children's attempts to organize and express their own information and interests as they write (Fearn & Farnan, 2001). The children in Grace's classroom, for example, responded to activities for rehearsal and peer-to-peer collaboration with heightened excitement, engagement, and growth. These activities supported their successful engagement as writers.

Systematic Observation

As described in Chapter 1, the overall purpose of systematic observation is to gather continuous and reliable information about children's current ways of working on literacy tasks, thus avoiding teaching based solely on assumptions or curricular sequences (Clay, 2013). Similar to the information obtained from running records, teachers need trustworthy information about children's writing: concepts about print, letter writing, strategies for word solving, self-monitoring and self-correction, oral language skills, and keeping their writing on track (Clay, 2014).

To gather such data, teachers can make a record capturing the observable problem-solving strategies and attempts a child utilizes for a chosen aspect of writing. A teacher might briefly observe a small group of students at work on their writing and make notes each time students seek some kind of support: "Andre turned to word wall to spell *maybe*, didn't find it, wrote a different word. Kerry, Clarice laughed together over Clarice's writing, Kerry suggested a next idea." Analysis of overall patterns in children's writing behaviors helps determine whether students are ready for a new challenge or are in need of reteaching. A teacher might discover, for example, that students' writing behavior demonstrates a need to teach for use of the word wall: "If you need to write a word like *maybe*, what smaller words could you look for on the word wall?"

Analytic assessment (Fearn & Farnan, 2001) is one type of informal assessment designed to help teachers understand children's current writing strengths and the results of recent writing instruction. Teachers can begin by making a list of key aspects of informational writing that have been taught recently. Then, they should collect a recent sample of each child's writing (from either the whole class or a small group) and construct a chart with a column for those aspects of writing recently taught and a row for each child. Teachers can use this chart to record the degree to which each child's writing demonstrates each skill.

Figure 5.4 illustrates an analytic assessment that would assist Grace in determining children's current instructional needs.

Given the information shown in the table, Grace would identify at least two students in need of immediate instructional support. Ira and Sato, in particular, would benefit from additional small-group instruction focused on oral rehearsal of the language needed for their writing. Grace would help these students incorporate couplet sentence structures into their writing. They might also benefit from several short collaborative writing sessions during work time or a shared writing activity with a classroom volunteer.

DEDICATED TIME FOR WRITING

There is an urgent need for significant time for writing instruction in K–2 classrooms. The U.S. Department of Education's *What Works Clearinghouse* review of research on writing instruction (Graham, Bollinger, Olson, D'Aoust, MacArthur, McCutchen, & Olinghouse, 2012) concluded that a minimum of 1 hour a day (30 minutes in kindergarten) should be devoted to writing instruction. Dedicating an hour each day for writing instruction in an already busy primary-grade classroom may sound like a daunting

Figure 5.4. Excerpt of Grace's Analytic Assessment

	Text: Included Related Title?	Fluency: # of Words Written	Content: # of Different Facts	Language: # of Couplets/ Total Sentences	Spelling: Full or Partial Phonetic Spelling?
Andrew	Yes	27	7	0/5	Full
Holly	Yes	42	9	5/5	Full
Ira	Yes	17	3	0/3	Partial
Sato	No	6	1	0/1	Partial
Matt	Yes	20	4	1/3	Partial

task. These recommended times, however, include prewriting, research, drafting, and revision, as well as discipline-specific writing.

Writing instruction should be integrated within mathematics, art, social studies, and reading instruction. Students might, for example, collaborate in small groups during work time or centers to write a report for an animal of their choice (as follow-up to the classroom instruction focused on foxes described earlier). Similarly, Dorn and Soffos (2012) recommended 90 minutes of Reading Workshop, 30 minutes of Language Workshop, 45 minutes of Writing Workshop, and 45 minutes of Content Workshop per day for K–3 students. In this model, writing activities are incorporated as an integral part of the learning in each block:

- *Reading Workshop:* Writing in journals as response to reading. This activity extends students' comprehension and reading engagement.
- *Language Workshop:* Writing in word study notebooks, providing practice using newly learned language, vocabulary, and writing skills.
- *Writing Workshop:* Participating in skills lessons to learn how to investigate, rehearse, draft, revise, edit, and share.
- *Content Workshop:* Engaging in writing-to-learn activities, to explain, describe, predict, and reflect on new learning through writing.

Frequent writing instruction allows teachers to be in good touch with children's current strength and weaknesses. Otherwise, both teacher and children will have to "restart" their learning each time a new lesson occurs. With frequent writing instruction, children are given time to put new learning into practice. They hear about a useful strategy or two, try these out right away in their own writing, receive guidance and support as they do so, and thus begin to internalize and apply strategies with growing independence.

SUMMARY

Grace's second writing lesson created an immediate "sea change" in student responses. Beginning with her introduction of verbal and visual note-taking, Grace's students engaged in a variety of prewriting activities with energy and interest. All children were observed to stretch their writing skills over several subsequent lessons, with extended composing and increasingly complex ideas and sentence structures. Matt began to write drafts of increasing length and with greater confidence. He also began to use writing strategies that he had previously abandoned in confusion.

The amount and intensity of instructional and peer support provided to Grace's students was multiplied several times over, providing extended opportunities to learn:

- multiple, collaborative opportunities for children to explore and talk about a topic in depth,
- immediate use of new learning in teacher- and peer-supported, independent writing, and
- targeted, differentiated assistance from a teacher who knows each child's current strength and difficulties in writing.

Figure 5.5 summarizes the chapter's recommendations in relationship to the CCSS.

FURTHER STUDY

Clay, M. M. (2001). Extra power from writing in early literacy interventions. In *Change over time in children's literacy development* (pp. 11–37). Portsmouth, NH: Heinemann.

> Study this chapter to learn more about Clay's understandings of the literacy processing used by young writers and the reciprocal relationship between learning to read and learning to write. This chapter would be an excellent choice for a voluntary professional study group, allowing team members to discuss a section or two of the chapter at a time and explore the concepts described by Clay within their own classrooms.

Gibson, S. A. (2008). An effective framework for primary-grade guided writing instruction. *The Reading Teacher, 62*(4), 324–334.

> This article describes the steps used to teach guided writing instruction for small groups of children. This instruction provides a bridge between whole-class writing lessons and children's use of writing strategies for their own, independent writing. The article emphasizes that children do not learn to write simply because they write each day, and it describes the teaching of writing strategies and coaching for students while they write.

Figure 5.5. Summary of Main Points: Learning to Write with Guidance and Support

Recommendations	Clay's Literacy Processing Theories (2014)	California Common Core State Standards
Implement frequent writing lessons and extended independent writing time.	Teaching improves when teachers understand children's strength and needs. Writers improve with time to put new learning into practice.	Kindergarten through 2nd-grade children write extended types of texts with guidance and support (CDE, 2014, p. 19).
Avoid mimicking or copying tasks for writing.	Young writers learn how to coordinate complex tasks of writing through multiple opportunities to learn within a rich instructional context.	Student growth in independence is valued; children become actively engaged, self-directed learners (CDE, 2014, p. 7).
Provide differentiated writing instruction.	Include rich, open tasks for accessing and organizing knowledge, rehearsal, and collaborative writing.	Instruction should be differentiated. Teach students what they need to learn and not what they already know (CDE, 2014, p. 15).
Teach so that children produce better drafts over time.	Children's successful text construction is a central cause of improvement in literacy processing.	The standards reflect an integrated model of literacy learning (CDE, 2014, p. 4).
Teach children how to give momentary attention to spelling strategies while writing.	Children need to put new and tentative strategies into practice when writing.	Foundational skills are not an end in and of themselves; they are the means with which children become proficient writers (CDE, 2014, p. 15).

CHAPTER 6

A Steep Gradient into More Complex Literacy Tasks

Grade-level (or higher) literacy achievement requires ongoing, fast-paced learning: "The teaching has to provide a gradient of difficulty in the tasks such that learners have many opportunities to try to work at higher levels of complexity" (Clay, 2001, p. 19). Teachers' expert presentation of new and achievable challenges provides the context within which children can extend their learning into more sophisticated use of concepts about print, knowledge of letter/letter sounds and words, language, meaning, and information. Clay (2005b) identified at least two ways in which this occurs: Children meet the challenges within new, appropriately difficult texts, and participate actively in a diverse range of effective instructional activities. K–2 literacy instruction, then, builds a strong foundation for children's accurate, fluent, enjoyable, and confident use of effective strategic activity.

This chapter offers examples and an explanation of the (1) rigor needed in K–2 classroom literacy programs, (2) changes that occur over time in children's literacy development, and (3) importance of both familiar and appropriately challenging text. We illustrate these principles with descriptions of one teacher's small-group reading instruction, fluency-oriented lessons, and vocabulary instruction for English language learners. Readers may want to consider the following focus questions while reading this chapter:

1. How is rigor achieved in K–2 literacy instruction?
2. What are the key differences between easy, familiar, instructional, frustration-level, and complex text?
3. How does frustration-level reading affect children's literacy processing and overall reading progress?
4. How do teachers know when to choose more complex text for instruction?
5. How can lessons in challenging texts be structured for successful, rigorous instruction?
6. What are effective ways to teach vocabulary to English language learners?

ENGINEERING A STEP UP IN COMPLEX LEARNING

The ELL students in one of Thomas's 2nd-grade reading groups were ready for additional challenge. These students were at an "Expanding" level of English language ability based on the California Department of Education's English language development standards; they were using English words and phrases with increasing fluency and ease, and needed moderate linguistic support when engaged in cognitively demanding activities (CDE, 2012). Thomas made the decision to implement additional challenge based on his observation of their confident and fluent reading in recent texts. His students also demonstrated basic understanding of events and explicit information, and they were beginning to ask their own questions about texts. Thomas's students, however, had difficulty understanding both vocabulary and inferential information. They often needed teacher assistance, for instance, to determine an author's main idea, or characters' reactions to events and problems.

Thomas chose *The Trail of Tears* (Bruchac, 1999) for this group's next text. This six-chapter literary nonfiction book describes the Cherokee's historic struggle to keep their homes, land, and self-government. The text uses short, succinct sentences, and presents information through both literary descriptions of characters and events and informational description of historical events. Thomas chose his teaching moves based on the book's historic setting, characterization, listing of dates and events, and episodic text structure. He determined that his students would need instructional support to infer the consequences of historical events and human motivations, and to decode and understand multisyllabic vocabulary.

Thomas began instruction with a brief description of the book's focus: "This book has information for us about the history of the Cherokee Indians. We will learn about the lives of the Cherokee and find out why they had to move many miles to other lands in the west." Thomas also discussed why readers should preview a new book before reading: to understand and gather information about a topic. As his students previewed the title, chapter headings, and pictures, he engaged them in relevant discussion and asked questions designed to spark active comprehension: "The word *civilized* means that a group of people are organized to live together with their own laws and beliefs. How might the author show us that the Cherokee people were civilized?" Thomas also provided background knowledge to help students understand the book's organization and graphics: "This map shows the part of America that the Cherokee lived in before our country's revolutionary war with England."

Thomas gave each student a "thinking card" to remind them of their learning goals (see Figure 6.1) and discussed this reminder briefly with the group.

Figure 6.1. Comprehension Thinking Card

As you read, think about:

1. The details from the story

2. What the author wants you to understand

He then asked his students to read the first chapter silently. As his students read independently, Thomas occasionally asked a student to either read a sentence or two aloud to him or comment on what he had just read. As students finished reading, they were asked to turn to a partner and read an important detail from the chapter out loud. Thomas highlighted several of these choices in discussion with the whole group: "Marie and Phuong chose the sentence, 'His people do not have enough food or blankets.' Why does the author want you to know this detail?" He also introduced a chart (see Figure 6.2) relating textual details to characters' motivations, and the group constructed one example together.

Thomas congratulated his students on their progress to a targeted goal: "Great work, everyone! You are learning how to think about what the details in a story tell you about the author's main ideas." Students then worked with a partner at their desks to complete at least two rows from the chart explaining the reactions of the Cherokee leader, John Ross, to events.

ACHIEVING RIGOR IN K–2 CLASSROOM LITERACY INSTRUCTION

As illustrated in Thomas's lesson, a rigorous K–2 literacy program provides in-depth, thoughtfully designed instruction targeted directly to children's best next steps. The goal is not to simply help children achieve some degree of progress. Instead, instruction moves students as quickly as possible to proficiency (or better). Thomas knew, for example, that his 2nd-grade students needed to extend their ability to use orthographic and phonological knowledge with a high degree of flexibility and efficiency, in order to keep their attention during reading on the messages of texts (Kaye, 2006). Clay (1991b) recommended a wide-ranging curriculum based on activities that are neither too limiting for children nor too difficult. This mix allows children to experience success (supported by instruction) on tasks that are increasingly complex and to construct a strong foundation that prevents later difficulties.

Teachers should increase the complexity and challenge of instructional goals, activities, and texts *as soon as* students' current literacy behaviors indicate that they are likely to be successful. The teacher thus raises the

Figure 6.2. Inferring Character Reactions (*The Trail of Tears*, Bruchac, 1999)

Character	What Does the Author Say?	What Does the Author Mean?
John Ross	• looked at his home for the last time. • thought of everything they were leaving behind them.	He is sad that they have to leave their home.

stakes for children as much as possible without causing confusion, and children's reading and writing behaviors should improve on a daily basis. Children cannot begin to construct the in-the-head processing needed for literacy learning until they engage in active thinking and use of strategic activities while reading and writing (Clay, 2001; Doyle, 2013). Children's reading of consistently easy texts during instruction may stall or slow their progress. Thomas, in contrast, engaged his students in cognitively challenging thinking in a subsequent lesson:

> ***Thomas:*** Let's practice using details to understand what the author wants us to know. How do we know that the Cherokee were treated badly?
>
> ***Ashlee:*** They had no clothes.
>
> ***Phuong:*** And nothing to cook in too.
>
> ***Thomas:*** Yes, they didn't have enough clothes to protect them from the sun or utensils to cook with. Those are good details. They help us understand how the Cherokee were treated. The government wanted to force the Cherokee people to move. The word *force* means to make someone do something even if they don't want to. Turn to your partner and think of a sentence with the words *Cherokee* and *force* in it. So [after listening to students' sentences] why did John Ross ask the government to let the Cherokee people travel to Oklahoma in their own way?
>
> ***Phuong:*** To not force them?
>
> ***Terrie:*** To make their own decisions.
>
> ***Ashlee:*** So it would be better for them.
>
> ***Thomas:*** Right. Turn to your partner and predict what will happen as the Cherokee people start on their journey. Remember to use what you already know about what happened to the Cherokee to make your prediction.

Rigorous instruction requires more rather than less instructional support. It also requires an instructional focus on children's thinking and problem solving—on their use of strategic activity to decode and comprehend text (Clay, 2001). Thomas, for example, supported his students' meaning-making as he taught them how to use inferencing and predicting strategies. He also provided linguistic information by expanding student answers and defining a challenging word. Thomas's students responded to his instruction with obvious engagement. They were confident that they would be successful in achieving the stated learning goals and were willing to focus their thinking in pursuit of this learning.

Understanding Text Complexity

A rigorous classroom literacy program is dependent, in part, on teachers' understanding of the varying characteristics and purposes of complex, frustration, instructional, familiar, and easy text. Rigorous instruction does not introduce children to complex ways of thinking while they are reading easy texts (Hiebert & Van Sluys, 2014). Instead, children learn how to use complex thinking while reading appropriately complex texts. Teachers, then, need to integrate their choice of challenging goals with instructionally appropriate texts. In the discussion below, we explain the differences between these five types of texts.

Complex Text. Text complexity is defined on a continuum of specific textual characteristics. Complex texts, for example, may present multiple levels of meaning, include more implicit information and sophisticated graphics, point to complex or multiple themes, or require understanding of discipline-specific knowledge (NGACBP & CCSSO, 2010). For young readers in particular, complex text may be written with longer and more complex sentence structures that are increasingly different from children's own oral language patterns (including "book-like" sentence structures, descriptive language, or dialogue), and sentences may extend beyond a single line of print. Most basal reading programs, however, do not present texts in a careful sequence of increasing complexity. Teachers should be able to analyze the types and amounts of complexity in each text, and choose texts for instruction from a variety of sources.

Frustration-Level Text. In contrast to complex text, frustration level describes a significant mismatch between a reader's current strengths and a text's specific characteristics (Clay, 1991a, 2005b). A more complex and challenging text may or may not be at frustration level for any individual child or group of children. Frustration level cannot be determined simply by the level of books that a child is currently reading in small-group or whole-class reading instruction. Teachers should assume, for example, that a child who has been reading texts with success in her reading group at any particular level might also be able to take on the challenges of texts at a higher level of complexity. Frustration-level texts are by definition simply too hard for a particular child to read. Frustration-level texts are so difficult, in fact, that no amount or type of teacher or peer support will allow the child to read with adequate decoding, fluency, and comprehension (Fountas & Pinnell, 2014). Although children do need to read (and write) increasingly complex and challenging texts, they do not need to read at frustration level. If forced to read such texts, beginning readers' processing breaks down into limited strategy use with little comprehension—or they simply attempt to memorize the text.

Figure 6.3 shows an excerpt of a child's reading of a frustration-level text. The child's attempts are shown above the line, with the text itself below the line.

The strategic activities attempted by this reader were broadly appropriate. She tried to identify words by using one or two letter sounds (e.g., *cat* for *can't*, *zoo* for *too*). She also monitored the sense of her reading, indicated

Figure 6.3. Example of Frustration-Level Reading Behaviors

Child:	No stop Laura [shakes head]
Text:	**"No," said Laura, sadly.**

Child:	Mops loves /m/ /m/ zoo?
Text:	**"Sally loves Mop, too.**

Child:	We cat [shakes head] ran.
Text:	**We can't keep her.**

/m/ -   Indicates child's articulation of the letter sound only.

Source: Giles (1997). *Just one guinea pig*. Crystal Lake, IL: Rigby.

in part by an interrogative voice after reading "Mops loves zoo." She was not able to determine for herself, however, whether these strategies actually work. Her errors allowed for limited understanding of the text at best—and by the third line in this sample, her reading did not maintain meaningful sentence structure. She thus lacked sufficient feedback to judge whether or not she had solved words correctly. Consequently, she began to simply skip words with a quick shake of her head. She may have begun to doubt the efficacy of the strategic activity she used in her attempts to decode and gain meaning from the text. This reader, then, lost ground in her development of processing strategies as a direct result of the confusion caused by this frustration-level text—putting her literacy progress at risk.

Frustration level cannot be determined simply by calculating the percent of words a child read correctly. The accuracy score is only an abbreviated method for *estimating* the degree to which a child has been able to identify high-frequency words, decode, and use strategic activities while reading. A low accuracy score, for instance, may occur because a child (1) read the text with very poor fluency, thus losing track of language and meaning; (2) made numerous errors on nonessential or repeating words; (3) made errors primarily on unknown, technical, or complex vocabulary; or (4) did not yet have the requisite background knowledge needed for the text's topic. It is probable that these types of difficulties could be ameliorated for children through intensive and carefully designed instruction. (Running record assessment, in fact, generally occurs *after* instruction and on a text that has already been read by the child at least once.) If instruction does not enable a child's successful problem solving of new challenges, however, the text may be at frustration level and should be avoided until the child's reading ability has improved.

Instructional-Level Text. Texts that are appropriate for instruction are "just challenging enough" (Robertson, Dougherty, Ford-Connors, & Paratore, 2014, p. 550). Children need to engage in complex thinking and successful solving of new words, with sufficient instructional support and within text that provides new, but doable, challenges (Clay, 1991a, 2005b). Thus, the teacher must provide information and modeling as needed to mediate children's reading and ensure successful learning. Instructional texts support teachers' ability to expand and solidify students' content knowledge, use of strategic activity, and positive responses to instruction (Fountas & Pinnell, 2014). Such instruction may include a teacher introduction to a new story, demonstration of monitoring or self-correction, and/or prompting for new decoding or comprehension strategies.

With careful observation of his students' reading behaviors, for example, Thomas selected and taught an appropriately challenging text to his students. Figure 6.4 illustrates his student Marie's reading behaviors from a portion of *The Trail of Tears* (Bruchac, 1999).

As Thomas listened to Marie's reading, he confirmed that she was able to read this text with successful problem solving. Marie corrected her initial error of *blanks* for the word *blankets*, for example, by using the text's meaning and all parts of the word in text. Marie (1) integrated meaning, language, and phonetic information to monitor, search for information, and self-correct as needed, and (2) read fluently and confidently.

Children are not expected to read instructional level text with 100% accuracy and fully accurate, high-level comprehension. Marie, for example, did not correct her error of *don't* for the words *do not*, and was not able to solve the word *sorrow*. It is likely, however, that *sorrow* was not known vocabulary for Marie. Beginning readers are generally not able to determine when they have solved a word correctly if they cannot match their decoding attempts to a word they already know. Thomas understood, then, that Marie's difficulty with this word indicated a continuing need for English vocabulary development. He also knew that Marie was easily familiar with the concept of sadness; *sorrow* was simply a new, English label for a known concept for Marie.

Typically, teachers will increase the text difficulty level used for instruction on at least a weekly basis. Children should thus be reading books during

Figure 6.4. Marie's Instructional-Level Reading Behaviors

Marie:	John Ross is /w/ worried. His per, people don't have
Text:	**John Ross is worried. His people do not have**

Marie:	ē, enough food or blanks, blankets. Many of them are will, ill.
Text:	**enough food or blankets. Many of them are ill.**

Marie:	All of them are /f/ ill, filled with [pause] sad. "No, I don't know."
Text:	**All of them are filled with sorrow.**

Source: Bruchac (1999). *The Trail of Tears*. New York, NY: Random House.

instruction that are consistently at the upper edge of their current learning (Fountas & Pinnell, 2012a). Children should read more complex text *as soon as they are able to do so successfully*. Teachers might decide when to increase the text difficulty level, for example, by establishing a clear target; teachers can identify a specific text that children will be able to read and comprehend within a few weeks (Calkins, Ehrenworth, & Lehman, 2012) and use this goal to establish specific instructional goals.

A fast pace of learning is not achieved when children read texts that are at the same level of difficulty for long periods. It is rarely appropriate, for example, to keep emergent readers in the easiest, levels A and B (Fountas & Pinnell, 2013) books for more than a few weeks. Children should be moved out of these earliest text levels as soon as they can match words one-to-one and accurately read several high-frequency words. This quick change in text level ensures that children have opportunities to identify more and more words within meaningful text, thus establishing their early and crucial monitoring. Similarly, Marie's reading of a more complex, grade 2 text (as in Figure 6.4 above) allowed her to successfully use parts of words to decode accurately and independently. English language learners (like all students) need instruction focused on learning targets and high expectations that acknowledge their capacity and interest in high-level thinking (CDE, 2012; Echevarria, Frey, & Fisher, 2015). Thomas's choice of text allowed Marie to participate in cognitively challenging discussions focused on character motivations and historical events. It is unlikely that she would have encountered these same types of opportunities in less complex text. When teachers fail to increase the difficulty level as children's knowledge and skills expand, they deny children the opportunities they need (in complex text, information, reasoning, and talk) to extend their learning.

When students seem to need to remain at an easier text level for a longer time frame, it is likely that instruction has not yet targeted their needs appropriately (Clay, 2005b). The teacher should consider how children could best learn to monitor and self-correct with greater sophistication, and what extra instructional work will be needed in order to move quickly into more difficult text (Clay, 2005a):

- Consider the current strengths of a group of children. What literacy- or discipline-related topics are they interested in, and what kinds of discussions about text best engage their interests? This information will help a teacher focus instruction on new, challenging text and interests.
- Take a running record (Clay, 2000a, 2013) with one or two children in a particular group on a slightly more challenging text.

Analyze the records to determine what strategic activities children are not yet using effectively. These strategies can then be taught in a series of intensive, targeted lessons in preparation for reading more challenging texts.

- Make a list of the texts that students in a small group have read over the past several weeks, along with brief teacher observations of the ease or particular difficulties children have encountered. Reflect on this information to consider what kinds of new challenges the group might take on successfully, and with what types of instructional support.

- Observe a child who is reading independently during a work-time activity. Consider the kinds of texts this child chooses to read in this context and observe her reading for signs of successful strategic activity. Consider how this information might point to a choice of more complex text during reading instruction.

Familiar and Easy Text. Beginning readers need to reread familiar texts for a variety of purposes and in differing contexts. Familiar texts are texts that a child can read with strong accuracy, fluency, and meaning making, based on instruction and the child's previous practice within the same text. Clay judged that two kinds of learning are needed for good progress: successful rereading of familiar books for fluent decisionmaking, and problem solving when reading new, instructional-level texts (Clay, 2005a). Books that a child has memorized, however, are no longer useful as familiar text. Instead, familiar books require children to "do some reading work, engaging with print, and picking up new information" (Clay, 2005b, p. 98). Children use their prior knowledge of each familiar text to read with greater independence, coordinating their practiced use of strategic activities in sustained and meaningful reading (Clay, 1991a).

Teachers can arrange for children to reread familiar texts in a variety of instructional contexts:

- rereading of texts that were taught in shared-reading lessons during work-time or center activities .
- echo or choral rereading with peers or classroom volunteers during work-time or center activities.
- rereading to family members for at-home practice.
- audio recording of rereading. The child might listen to her recorded reading, and perhaps rerecord for better fluency if needed.
- rereading that occurs as children arrive at the start of the school day or after recess.

Easy texts are those that a child can already read at very high levels of accuracy, good fluency, and strong comprehension with few (if any) difficulties and no instructional support from teachers or peers. Easy texts do not generally need to be addressed within reading instruction. Instead, children typically choose these texts themselves for enjoyment or their own interests, or as models or sources of information for research and writing projects.

TEACHING FOR SUCCESSFUL READING OF INCREASINGLY COMPLEX TEXT

Children's word reading and comprehension skills improve when the amount of time they spend reading complex text is increased (Kuhn, Schwanenflugel, Morris, Morrow, Woo, Meisinger, . . . Stahl, 2006). Teachers need to (1) have faith in the ability of children to become proficient readers and writers when provided with sufficient instructional guidance, and (2) develop wide and deep expertise in techniques used to introduce children to new learning and guide them as they learn strategic activity. The following sections describe instructional activities that provide rigorous support for children's stretch into complex literacy tasks: whole-class fluency-oriented instruction and vocabulary instruction for English language learners.

Fluency-Oriented Reading Instruction

Fluency-oriented reading instruction (FORI; Stahl & Heubach, 2005) is a version of shared reading designed specifically to build readers' success in challenging texts. The shared reading described in Chapter 2 of this book illustrates teaching for emergent readers' understanding of early behaviors and concepts about print. FORI, in contrast, targets students' detailed, high-level comprehension and wide reading of increasingly sophisticated texts. We recommend FORI only for children who have already progressed beyond an emergent level of reading development. Such children are at a strong mid-1st- or 2nd-grade reading level (or higher) and are transitioning to faster processing while reading and writing.

FORI improves children's reading of challenging texts (Kuhn & Schwanenflugel, 2006; Rasinski, Reutzel, Chard, & Linan-Thompson, 2011), but does not replace small-group instruction or independent reading. FORI lessons take no more than 30 minutes each day. Each student must have his own copy of the text, and teachers choose sufficiently complex text from a variety of sources (such as a basal reading program or trade books). The teacher begins the weeklong FORI instructional cycle on a new text with an introduction and read-aloud. Figure 6.5, for example, lists possible techniques to ensure students' comprehension *before and during* the teacher's initial reading of *One Morning in Maine* (McCloskey, 1952).

These activities are brief, so that the teacher's reading of the text is sustained and fluent. Immediately *after* the first reading, the teacher leads a discussion focused on comprehension. The teacher might, for example, ask an inferential or application-level question and allow time for students to support their responses with reference to specific portions of the text. Student partners, then, can take a few minutes to highlight a relevant detail or two from the text, and explain to each other how these support their thinking.

During the next 4 days, the teacher reintroduces the text to students each day (perhaps revisiting instructional goals or reviewing information for students from an already completed graphic organizer). Students then reread this same text, using one of the following activities each day:

- *Echo reading.* The teacher reads a section of the text, and students then echo-read that same section chorally. Echo reading can begin with just one or two sentences at a time and proceed to full paragraphs when students are successful.
- *Choral reading.* The whole class reads either all or a portion of the text together. Teachers should use their own voice to direct the pace and fluency of students' choral reading. This reading must not be allowed to degrade into a slow, word-by-word pace, or be conducted without appropriate expression and phrasing. If needed, the teacher can stop the reading to demonstrate how it should sound before continuing.
- *Partner reading.* Students take turns reading the text with either a self- or teacher-selected partner. The partner will simply tell a difficult word to his or her peer as needed, without comment or teaching. Students generally read a paragraph or page before the partner takes a turn (rather than trading turns sentence by sentence). This structure allows each partner sufficient time in sustained reading.
- *Radio reading* (Searfoss, 1975). Students, in small groups or with partners, practice reading an appropriate portion of the text so that a listener would understand the text's meaning. Partners can improve their fluency by audio recording and then listening to ensure that the reading is comprehensible.
- *Take-home reading.* Students are typically asked to read the same text at home each week.

Figure 6.5. Developing Students' Comprehension During Fluency-Oriented Reading Instruction

Instructional Techniques (*One Morning in Maine*, McCloskey, 1952)	
Preparing to read:	
Main idea/purpose statement	"As you listen to this story, make sure you understand what the setting is and why Sal is so worried."
Teacher's own response to the text	"When I read this story, I loved learning about digging up clams. I also laughed at some of the things that Sal talked about!"
"As you study this book you will learn how to . . .	
Decoding	read longer words, like *swallowed* and *certainly*."
Fluency	read dialogue with expression and phrasing so that it sounds like people are talking."
Comprehension	describe a theme the author wrote about and what details from the text support the theme."
Teacher's think-aloud during reading:	
Vocabulary	"Oh! The loon ate a herring whole. I think herring must be a kind of fish."
Inferential information	"I think she is pretending that she isn't really crying, though."
Text structure	"The next part of the story is a different episode, since Sal has finished getting ready and is on her way to help her father dig clams. Let's see what happens."

All students should learn how to read the text with reasonable accuracy and strong fluency. The intent is *not*, however, for students to either memorize a text or read at 100% accuracy (even proficient readers make errors from time to time). Instead, students' reading should simply be at a good pace and with appropriate phrasing, expression, and comprehension.

Teaching Vocabulary to English Language Learners

Effective vocabulary instruction for English language learners is thorough and explicit. Children need multiple exposures to target words and should practice speaking, reading, and writing with these same words for several days (Gersten, Baker, Shanahan, Linan-Thompson, Collins, & Scarcella, 2007). They also need to engage in rich discussions that help them connect new words or concepts to prior knowledge (Ganske & Jocius, 2013). Students do not, however, need to learn the meanings of all unfamiliar words in a text. Instead, the focus is on in-depth instruction for words most essential to students' ability to understand and talk about the story. In addition, a strategic approach teaches children how to problem-solve word meanings with growing independence. This dual approach acknowledges that children have strengths they can use for vocabulary learning; they have been learning new language structures, concepts, and words since birth. Clay (2001, 2014) believed that it is important to build new learning on children's strengths. Encouraging children to guess or estimate a challenging word's meaning (and treating those guesses as good thinking), for example, allows children to value and use their existing knowledge (O'Leary, 2009).

Thomas knew that his ELL students would encounter vocabulary challenges as they read *The Trail of Tears* (Bruchac, 1999). His students needed instructional assistance to decode and understand word meanings for the more complex concepts and multisyllabic words in this text. When his students had difficulty understanding the word *belongings*, for example, Thomas reread a short section of the text containing the word and asked his students to estimate the word's meaning:

> ***Thomas:*** The book tells us that the Cherokee have finished packing their belongings, and it is time to go on their journey. Can you guess what the word *belongings* might mean?
>
> ***Phuong:*** All their things, to go with them?
>
> ***Terrie:*** Their clothes and stuff.
>
> ***Thomas:*** Let's see. Would *all of their things* make sense? All around him, other Cherokee have finished packing all of their things. How about *their clothes and stuff*? Other Cherokee have finished packing their clothes and stuff. Yes. Your guesses are very good, because you understand what the author has told you about this event. What information do you see inside the word, *belongings*, to help you understand what it means?
>
> ***Ashlee:*** It says *be* here.
>
> ***Terrie:*** And *belong*.
>
> ***Thomas:*** Yes. It makes sense that these things *belong* to them—their *belongings*. Good thinking, everyone.

Thomas began the discussion with an open-ended question to jump-start his students' thinking (Ganske & Jocius, 2013) and support their willingness to unpack word meanings. He also illustrated the use of strategies to determine a word's meaning.

Activities that are structured so children can revisit unfamiliar vocabulary in novel ways will reinforce new learning (August, McCardle, & Shanahan, 2014). A brief, focused instructional sequence for teaching vocabulary, for example, might include the following steps (Beck, McKeown, & Kucan, 2002; Manyak, Von Gunten, Autenrieth, Gillis, Mastre-O'Farrell, Irvine-McDermott, Baumann, & Blachowicz, 2014):

1. Introduce the new word in context: "In *The Trail of Tears*, the Cherokee families have packed their belongings."
2. Provide a child-friendly definition of the new word: "Belongings are the things that someone has or owns."
3. Explore multiple examples of the word beyond the context of the story. Children might, for example, remember packing their own belongings for a trip. Or, they might list or draw the belongings of a favorite story character.
4. Prompt children to describe the word's use from their own experiences: "What are some of your own favorite belongings? Why are they important to you?"
5. Ask a "thought question" (Manyak et al., 2014): "Do you think it is fair that some people have more belongings than others?"

Formal, dictionary definitions are generally not helpful for children—and simply copying these definitions is even less useful. This is especially true for English language learners (Gersten et al., 2007). Child-friendly definitions, in contrast, use language and examples that connect children's known concepts to target words (Beck, McKeown, & Kucan, 2002). The word *journey*, then, might be defined as follows: "A journey is a long and dangerous trip. Someone might go on a journey by riding his bike all the way to the grocery store." Language is also learned through conversation with others; children expand their own language by working to communicate important ideas and information and listening to how others respond. After an introduction to a new word, for example, students can create their own definitions. This can be accomplished in a shared writing activity, with children contributing ideas and helping with composition while the teacher transcribes on an easel or document viewer. Or, children can compose definitions as a center or work-time activity.

Children need to comprehend text with increasing independence, in part by learning useful strategic activities for problem-solving word meanings. In many cases, children will at least recall having heard or seen a particular word before. Students may be able, for example, to make broad guesses about a word as a useful, problem-solving strategy:

• "Do you think this might be something you would like, or not like?"
• "What idea does this word remind you of?"

Children may also be able to use cognates from their first language knowledge to define English words; the Spanish word *historia* can help children understand the English word *history*. Learning how to look for known parts of words is another effective strategy. Children may already know the meaning of one or more parts of a word (such as *belong* in *belongings*), thus giving them a starting point to solve the word's meaning: "What can you see [in that word] that might help?" (Clay, 2005b, p. 132). Teachers can demonstrate this strategy by using a finger or masking card to uncover known parts of a difficult word.

SUMMARY

Learning how to help young readers and writers progress up a steep gradient of difficulty is a challenging accomplishment. Implementing instruction that recognizes children's strengths and builds stronger levels of instructional support for more complex tasks typically requires the development of expertise and collaboration with colleagues. The following bullets summarize key points we have made in this chapter. Gathering a group of interested colleagues together for collaborative study focused on one or two of these points will help to ensure that children learn at a fast rate of progress:

- Rigorous literacy instruction requires both complex thinking and complex texts, balanced by the level and types of instructional support needed for children's successful processing.
- Helping children achieve some degree of progress is not sufficient in effective literacy instruction. Instead, rigorous instruction moves children to proficiency as fast as possible without causing confusion or a loss of self-efficacy.
- Children should not be reading texts for instruction at the same level of difficulty week after week.
- Children are not required to read text at 100% accuracy (although they will sometimes do so when reading self-chosen, easy text independently).
- There is no good reason for K–2 children to read frustration-level text. Instructional-level texts, however, must present sufficient challenges to drive children's learning.

FURTHER STUDY

Clay, M. M. (2001). Acts of literacy processing: An unusual lens. In *Change over time in children's literacy development* (pp. 39–90). Portsmouth, NH: Heinemann.

This chapter reviews Clay's findings regarding the changes that are seen in children's literacy processing over time. Clay described how children's reading behaviors and cognitive work alters as they learn to relate one thing to another and transition to faster processing. Clay also integrated this description of change over time with the need for children to experience rapid, successive changes in their literacy understandings. Studying the information in this chapter with particular children's progress in mind will help teachers consider what children most need to learn in order to progress at a faster pace of change.

O'Leary, S. (2009). Teaching essential vocabulary to English language learners. In C. Rodriguez-Eagle (Ed.). *Achieving success with English language learners: Insights, assessment, instruction* (pp. 125–142). Worthington, OH: Reading Recovery Council of North America.

This is an inspiring description of the author's collaborative study of vocabulary instruction for English language learners. O'Leary illustrated a team study of children's vocabulary learning, combined with the lessons she and her colleagues learned as this information was put into practice with children. Study this chapter to learn more about children's vocabulary learning, and for an excellent example of teacher professional development and collaborative learning.

Leadership in Classroom-Based Instructional Change

The challenge of literacy improvement is fine-tuning programs that are already satisfactory to get better results. . . . When you are doing a job like literacy teaching well, it is hard to think about doing it even better. (Clay, 2014, p. 211)

The links in this book between Clay's literacy processing theory and effective K–2 classroom instruction incorporate complex and challenging shifts in teaching structures and decisions—shifts that will engage both novice and experienced teachers in new learning across their teaching careers. Each of our readers will have no doubt found aspects of instruction in this book that they already understand well and that are fully implemented in their current instructional practices. Readers will also, we believe, have encountered principles and teaching practices in this book that can serve as a catalyst for change.

In this epilogue, we discuss how teachers can take action based on Clay's principles and our instructional recommendations. We conceptualize such decisions as a strategic choice: What starting point(s) might be a best choice for teachers of varying expertise and experience? We also discuss the (1) inquiry processes that might be used to guide teachers' change processes, and (2) how classroom teachers can exert leadership from within their own instructional practices and collaborative work with colleagues.

BUILDING A COMPREHENSIVE LITERACY PROGRAM ONE SHIFT AT A TIME

Clay's research and theories provide a solid, lasting foundation on which to build deep understanding of both children's literacy development and effective instruction. Clay (2014) believed that satisfactory progress after several years of school is exemplified by children who

- are eager to talk, read, and write,
- have developed a literacy-learning system for reading and writing a variety of texts,
- are learning how to read by reading; they self-monitor, search for more information, and self-correct,
- read and write many words quickly and know how to problem-solve new words, and
- have developed biliteracy when appropriate. (p. 215)

These results are at risk, however, when instruction is driven entirely by a sequenced curriculum, when children are not taught how to use strategic activity to read and write continuous text, when instruction is not appropriately differentiated, or when instruction does not provide consistent and appropriate levels of challenge.

It would be overwhelming to simply try to adhere immediately and fully to each of the principles of effective literacy instruction described in this book. Teachers' learning, in any case, is most powerful and long lasting when it is constructed over time and based on knowledge of accurate and comprehensive theories. The Consortium for Policy Research in Education (May, Sirinides, Gray, & Goldsworthy, 2016) found that effective, deliberate teaching depends on teachers' purposeful analysis of students' progress, ongoing reflection on their own teaching, and active engagement in continual learning. Strategic change is a deliberate and thoughtful restructuring of teacher knowledge and instructional contexts, and tightly connected to support for children's strong literacy progress. Exemplary teachers, for instance, report that they improved their own instructional practice one bit at a time over many years, typically beginning with in-depth study of a particular instructional activity (Day, 2001). Teachers will also be best able to support integrated literacy intervention for students in need (such as Reading Recovery instruction) when they develop their own strong understanding of effective instruction. Teachers' understanding of the comprehensive instruction recommended by Clay's theories, then, might be initiated with four self-directed questions:

1. How do Clay's theories best help me to understand how well my students are constructing processes for literacy learning?
2. How might I adapt my instruction, based on Clay's theories, to meet the needs of the children I am teaching now?
3. What instructional activity should I focus on as a starting point to improve my interaction with children?
4. In what ways do I most need to expand my own instructional expertise?

Gathering Data in Support of Change. Teacher learning and positive instructional change are best supported by teachers' own informal assessment. A self-inventory, for example, of their own current classroom instruction and children's responses is likely to point teachers to the most productive, possible areas for change in their own classrooms. One or more of the following questions might be used for a self-inventory:

- What is going well for my students during literacy instruction?
- What types of instruction seem to be consistently driving children's literacy learning in my classroom?
- When are the children I teach most successfully engaged in literacy tasks?
- What recent texts have been of best help to children's growth in reading and writing in my classroom?
- What are the strengths in the ways that the children I teach collaborate with one another during literacy learning?

Taking the time to reflect on successes helps teachers identify their instructional strengths. Of course, this reflection often leads teachers to question whether some particular aspects of their literacy instruction are as powerful as is needed. To study this question further, a classroom's literacy instruction might be considered from the viewpoint of a few children (perhaps a strong, an average, and a struggling reader):

- What specific learning opportunities has this child participated in this week? Has this learning occurred in whole-class, small-group, and individual contexts?
- Is this child reading (and writing) sufficient amounts and types of continuous text during literacy instruction? What kinds of text does he/she read (or write), and for how long each day?
- Does this child use strategies when reading? Is he or she learning more about how language and information work in print at an appropriate pace of change?
- What kinds of literacy growth have been observed for this child over the past week or 2? Did this child make any recent "ah-ha!" discoveries about how reading or writing works?

Teachers should seek evidence in support of any hunches arising from these questions. They can use informal assessment to inform moment-by-moment instructional decisions: "knowing what a child can almost do, can do independently, or in collaboration, or understands incompletely" (Johnston, 2003, p. 91). They might also use a basic question to determine what informal data is needed: "What information will help me know how well this child is able to . . . " To learn about a particular child's recent literacy growth, or types of strategies used by a child when reading, running record assessment (Clay, 2000a, 2013) will be of help. Or, a teacher might decide to informally "shadow" one child for a day or 2 by making occasional notes during the day on texts the child is reading, or groups the child participates in.

Prioritizing Needed Changes in Teacher Expertise and Instruction. Strategic change requires a focus on one or two priority areas that are in need of change. These priorities should be determined primarily by teachers' deliberate search to understand children's needs in light of Clay's theories. The identification of a priority for shifts in instruction will also differ based on each teacher's personal choice and interests, teaching experience, previous learning from self-directed inquiry and study, and participation in professional development and collaboration with colleagues. An increase in teacher knowledge and resulting instructional shifts do not, in any case, need to be implemented across the board. Wold (2002), for example, studied the deep-level learning and substantial changes in knowledge of three literacy teachers. These teachers built change into their practice over time in incremental ways:

> The smallest change is real when it occurs within actual teaching contexts and results in teachers' adding up information and improving practice over years of teaching. (Wold, 2002, p. 86)

Several possible starting points for teachers' inquiry and shifts in instruction are described below. Each of these is intended to further teachers' own learning and apply Clay's theories to classroom instruction, and was addressed in one or more chapters in this book. Choosing one or two of the following goals will allow teachers to focus on powerful, differentiated instruction for children's literacy processing:

1. Expand your knowledge of particular instructional activities. Use only those activities and instructional approaches, however, that truly help the children in *your* classroom learn.
   - Redesign reading lessons using varying structures and goals, as needed for those children who are struggling with reading proficiency or who are already strong readers.
   - Revise your use of instructional time to ensure that English language learners have extended time to engage in in-depth, focused discussion in order to expand their use of academic language.

2. Based on children's needs, design instruction as either brief, explicit demonstration or more extensive instructional conversation.

   - Learn how to lead instructional conversations in ways that ensure that students' on-topic ideas and contributions are valued and built on by your responses and in their interaction with peers.
   - Implement instruction to help the children in your classroom become better listeners during instructional conversations.

3. Learn more about teaching for children's use of strategic activity to ensure that they learn how to (1) self-monitor, search for information, and self-correct, and (2) monitor their understanding and comprehend text.

   - Practice using clear, direct language to prompt children to monitor their reading, or use strategies to decode difficult words.
   - Learn how to use verbal description effectively to provide teacher think-aloud for children's comprehension of both narrative and informational text.

4. Expand your understanding of instructional scaffolding: Why is it needed when children attempt challenging new learning?

   - Design and try out various ways to introduce new texts to children, depending on the level of support children need.
   - Practice techniques to help children in your classroom rehearse complex language structures before writing.

5. Reorganize your classroom schedule to support differentiated instruction, including lots of time for the children you teach to read and write continuous text.

   - Review your daily schedule to determine how much time is currently allowed for children's reading and writing. Increase this amount of time by integrating literacy instruction within other subject areas.
   - Evaluate how much classroom time you are using to teach in whole-class lessons. Consider whether some portions of this time need to be replaced with small-group instruction.

6. Learn how to teach children to stay engaged during independent work-time or center activities, leaving time for you to teach small groups and provide occasional brief coaching for individual children.

   - Visit with a colleague who has designed a set of high-quality work-time activities or centers for children. Consider how to adapt these for your own teaching.
   - Ask one of your colleagues who has particular expertise in teaching math (or any other subject area) to help you design a work-time center that integrates literacy with an authentic disciplinary task.

7. Practice one or two techniques for systematic observation in your classroom, and use the results to determine specific instructional goals for particular children.

- Find an expert on running record assessment who will share his or her knowledge with you, and begin practicing this technique in your classroom.
- Try out analytic assessment of children's writing. Use the results to understand what the children you teach have learned about writing from your recent instruction.

These are key options based on our understanding of priorities for effective classroom instruction. Readers may, of course, have developed additional interests and priorities from the material in this book.

Teachers who feel ready for further change and deep learning might focus on one or two of the suggestions below. These suggestions move beyond *teacher* actions to adaptive teaching based on noticing and interpretation of *children's* thinking (Gibson & Ross, 2016; Jacobs, Lamb, Philipp, & Schappelle, 2011).

1. Talk briefly with an individual child or two in your classroom. Ask the child to describe his thinking about the work he is doing.

- Reflect on your teaching strengths based on the child's thinking. How might you share these strengths with your colleagues?
- Use this information to identify a specific goal: In what ways might children's thinking change or be expanded over the next few days?

2. Use informal systematic observation to understand how the children in your classroom are learning, and compare their progress to Clay's description of the ways that high-progress readers and writers learn strategies and develop skills.

- Implement your detailed knowledge of children's reading and writing behaviors to teach lessons with a high density of instruction; address multiple goals in each lesson for children's best progress.
- Consider how you might teach your students to read and write with greater independence.

3. Fine-tune your coaching of individual children to best support their use of effective strategies as they read and write text.

- Consider how to maximize time in the classroom to allow for brief, but regularly occurring, opportunities for you to coach individual children as needed during reading and writing activities.

- Set a goal describing one child's expected learning over the next few days. Consider how you will prompt or coach that child to help him or her achieve the goal.

4. Create units of study to integrate children's disciplinary learning with literacy instruction.

   - Find a group of colleagues who are interested in collaborating with you to design a themed unit of study using a variety of types of informational texts.
   - As you design the unit, consider how children will best engage in tasks that expand their knowledge, interests, and thinking.

5. Determine how to help children in your classroom learn through new challenges and more complex text without frustration or confusion.

   - Explore specific ways to maintain a fast pace of change in children's learning from one day to the next in your classroom literacy instruction.
   - Study one child's (or group of children's) progress in depth by presenting a set of increasingly difficult challenges over several days and assisting as needed for success. What kinds of "stretch" was the child capable of achieving?

COLLABORATIVE EXTENDED LEARNING THROUGH CLASSROOM TEACHING

Exemplary teaching does not just happen naturally for a few "gifted" teachers. Instead, teachers develop expertise by becoming insightful observers of children while they are at work on literacy tasks, and by working with colleagues to make sense of these observations (Ross & Gibson, 2010). This is a continuous process of refining teaching over time with the needs of children firmly at the center of the learning.

It is common, in our experience, for classroom teachers to assert that they do not have the authority to engage in instructional leadership. Instructional leadership, however, does not arise primarily from authority (or solely from a position such as principal or literacy coach). Instead, effective K–2 classroom literacy teaching is a shared responsibility. Classroom teachers, in fact, are uniquely situated to both build and share knowledge with colleagues. They are actively engaged each day in fine-tuning their instruction on a moment-by-moment basis, and have immediate access to the information that best defines children's learning. This might include:

- descriptions of a child's current reading and writing behaviors,

- knowledge of the ability of particular children to function independently during literacy tasks,
- the strategies a child uses to attempt to decode or spell a difficult word,
- how well a child works to read and comprehend both narrative and informational text at varying levels of complexity, and
- knowing what particular work-time tasks best capture a child's sustained interest and results in a fast pace of learning.

This type of information is much more useful for immediate fine-tuning of instruction than test scores. Teachers' judgments about children's achievement levels are, in any case, in strong agreement with standardized achievement scores (Hoge & Coladarci, 1989). Moreover, teachers' day-to-day noticing provides a much needed, more immediate view of children's learning.

Classroom teachers, then, can engage in highly beneficial literacy leadership by conducting and sharing their learning and growth in tight connection to their own instructional practices. This in-depth knowledge of children's development and instruction is both verified and expanded through collaboration with colleagues. Engaging in one or more of the following suggestions will be a great start for teachers' leadership in classroom instruction:

1. Share what you are learning with colleagues. You do not need to be an expert, or have answers for all questions. Sharing your tentative, ongoing thinking and learning helps you to be more successful and will build a learning community within your grade level or school.

2. Ask tentative, nuanced, and important questions to spark other educators' interest and reflection:

   - "I've been thinking about the strengths in the ways we are teaching letter knowledge to children. It seems to be going very well, but I wonder if there are gaps in our teaching that we should consider to make our curriculum even better."
   - Help your colleagues consider which programs and approaches are actually working for your students. The practice guides or intervention reports from the *What Works Clearinghouse* (available at http://ies.ed.gov/ncee/wwc/) provide comprehensive, research-based information on the effectiveness of many such programs and can help you decide what you need to know about your own students' progress.

3. Find a small group of colleagues who are interested in meeting perhaps once a month to study and discuss a resource of interest:

   - any of the resources listed in the Further Study and Suggested Readings sections in this book
   - videos demonstrating particular aspects of effective literacy instruction from http://fdf.readingrecovery.org/

4. Invite a colleague to view a lesson (either in person or by video) or review your lesson plan for an instructional activity that you are working to expand and improve. Invite that colleague to provide you with suggestions.

5. Find and participate in high-quality staff development, university programs, or workshops. Choose only those activities that will explain the reasons or theories that lie behind any recommended methods or instructional approaches (Day, 2001) so that you can compare these with what you already know about how children develop literacy proficiency.

Everyone benefits when teachers, both as individual classroom teachers and in collaboration with colleagues, roll up their sleeves and work together to fine-tune instruction. Teachers pull together their own expertise and colleagues' varying viewpoints to best understand how students are progressing, design and fine-tune instruction, and construct a variety of instructional contexts to support appropriately differentiated literacy instruction with a focus on children's strategic activity. This professional level of interaction and commitment puts Clay's literacy processing theories to work in classroom instruction on behalf of children's strong progress as readers and writers.

Further Study

Askew, B. J., Pinnell, G. S., & Scharer, P. L. (2014). *Promising literacy for every child: Reading Recovery® and a comprehensive literacy system.* Worthington, OH: The Reading Recovery Council of North America. Available at www.readingrecovery.org

> This publication provides suggestions and self-evaluative frameworks to assist grade-level teams, schools, and districts as they consider what is happening already in literacy programs and what improvements are needed. The framework for self-evaluation of primary-grade literacy instruction, for example, addresses expertise, instruction, implementation, and accountability. The authors present points for reflection such as:
>
> - Do teachers have scheduled opportunities to collaborate and build expertise as a professional learning community?

- Does instruction include an appropriate use of whole-group, small-group, and individual settings to meet students' needs?
- Do students engage in extensive experiences in reading continuous text at the appropriate level of difficulty?

Day, J. P. (2001). How I became an exemplary teacher. (Although I'm really still learning just like anyone else.). In M. Pressley, R. L., Allington, R. Wharton-MacDonald, C. Collins-Block, & L. M. Morrow (Eds.), *Learning to read: Lessons from exemplary first-grade classrooms* (pp. 205–218). New York, NY: Guilford.

Day provides an important description of the ways that exemplary teachers changed their instructional practices over time and what the teachers themselves believed influenced their shifts in instruction. The author presents quotes from teachers' talk about their own learning and discusses categories of responses. Many of the teachers, for example, recommended that educators should "observe children and never stop learning" (p. 210).

Suggested Readings

Clay's Literacy Processing Theories:

Clay, J. (2009). *Memories of Marie Clay: Reflections on the life and work of Marie Clay*. Portsmouth, NH: Heinemann.

Clay, M. M. (1987). Learning to be learning disabled. *New Zealand Journal of Educational Studies, 22*(2), 155–173.

Clay, M. M. (2001). *Change over time in children's literacy development*. Portsmouth, NH: Heinemann.

Doyle, M. A. (2013). Marie M. Clay's theoretical perspective: A literacy processing theory. In D. E. Alvermann, N. J. Unrau, & R. B. Ruddell (Eds.), *Theoretical models and processes of reading* (pp. 636–656). Newark, DE: International Reading Association. Available as a single chapter from www.literacyworldwide. org/get-resources/books/710

Gaffney, J. S., & Askew, B. J. (Eds.). (1999). *Stirring the waters: The influence of Marie Clay*. Portsmouth, NH: Heinemann.

McNaughton, S. (2014). Classroom instruction: The influences of Marie Clay. *The Reading Teacher, 69*(2), 88–92.

Pinnell, G. S., & Fountas, I. C. (2006). Marie M. Clay: Demonstrating that the world can be different. *Language Arts, 83*(4), 364–370.

Vellutino, F. R. (2010). "Learning to be learning disabled": Marie Clay's seminal contribution to the response to intervention approach to identifying specific reading disability. *The Journal of Reading Recovery, 10*(1), 5–23.

Clay's Theories of Writing Development:

Clay, M. M. (1975). *What did I write? Beginning writing behaviour*. Portsmouth, NH: Heinemann.

Clay, M. M. (2001). Extra power from writing in early literacy interventions. In *Change over time in children's literacy development*. Portsmouth, NH: Heinemann.

Clay, M. M. (2010). *How very young children explore writing*. Portsmouth, NH: Heinemann.

Clay, M. M. (2012). What changes in writing can I see? *Language Arts, 89*(3), 195–196.

Clay, M. M. (2014). Fostering independence in writing. In *By different paths to common outcomes: Literacy learning and teaching* (pp. 177–185). Auckland, New Zealand: The Marie Clay Literacy Trust.

Clay, M. M. (2014). The power of writing in early literacy. In *By different paths to common outcomes: Literacy learning and teaching* (pp. 145–176). Auckland, New Zealand: The Marie Clay Literacy Trust.

Clay, M. M. (2014). Talking, reading, and writing. In *By different paths to common outcomes: Literacy learning and teaching* (pp. 122–144). Auckland, New Zealand: The Marie Clay Literacy Trust.

Systematic Observation of Children's Literacy Behaviors:

Clay, M. M. (2000a). *Running records for classroom teachers.* Portsmouth, NH: Heinemann.

Clay, M. M. (2000b). *Concepts about print: What have children learned about the way we print language?* Portsmouth, NH: Heinemann.

Clay, M. M. (2013). *An observation survey of early literacy achievement* (3rd ed.). Portsmouth, NH: Heinemann.

Clay, M. M., Gill, M., Glynn, T., McNaughton, T., & Salmon, K. (1983). *Record of oral language and biks and gutches.* Portsmouth, NH: Heinemann.

Comprehensive Literacy Instruction:

Askew, B. J., Pinnell, G. S., & Scharer, P. L. (2014). Promising literacy for every child: Reading Recovery® and a comprehensive literacy system. Worthington, OH: The Reading Recovery Council of North America. Available at www.readingrecovery.org

Dorn, L. J., & Soffos, C. (2012). *Interventions that work: A comprehensive intervention model for preventing reading failure in grades K–3.* Boston, MA: Pearson Education.

Lyons, C. A., & Pinnell, G. S. (2001). *Systems for change in literacy education.* Portsmouth, NH: Heinemann.

Primary-Grade Literacy Instruction:

Center for Early Literacy Information. [An online database of early literacy articles and information.] The Reading Recovery Council of North America. Available at www.earlyliteracyinfo.org/index.aspx

Clay, M. M. (2010). *The puzzling code.* Portsmouth, NH: Heinemann.

Clay, M. M. (2014). Introducing storybooks to young readers. In *By different paths to common outcomes: Literacy learning and teaching* (pp. 186–199). Auckland, New

Zealand: The Marie Clay Literacy Trust. (Also available as Clay, M. M. (1991). Introducing a new storybook to young readers. *The Reading Teacher*, 45(4), 264.)

Early Literacy Intervention: Expanding expertise and impact. Professional development resources to strengthen early literacy outcomes. [Online webcasts and other resources.] The Reading Recovery Council of North America. Available at fdf.readingrecovery.org

Effective literacy practices video library. The Reading Recovery Council of North America. Available at fdf.readingrecovery.org/resources/138

Fountas, I. C., & Pinnell, G. S. (2012a). Guided reading: The romance and the reality. *Reading Teacher*, 66(4), 268–284.

Fountas, I. C., & Pinnell, G. S. (2012b). *Prompting guides. Part 1 for oral reading and early writing*. Portsmouth, NH: Heinemann.

Fountas, I. C., & Pinnell, G. S. (2012c). *Prompting guides. Part 2 for comprehension*. Portsmouth, NH: Heinemann.

Gibson, S. A. (2008). An effective framework for primary-grade guided writing lessons. *The Reading Teacher*, 62(4), 324–334.

Gibson, S. A. (2010). Strategy guide: Shared writing. ReadWriteThink: International Reading Association. Retrieved from www.readwritethink.org/professional-development/strategy-guides/shared-writing-30686.html

Gibson, S. A. (2010). Strategy guide: Write alouds. ReadWriteThink: International Reading Association. Retrieved from www.readwritethink.org/professional-development/strategy-guides/write-alouds-30687.html

Gibson, S. A. (2012). Teaching vocabulary: High student engagement in text and talk. *The California Reader*, 45(2), 5–10.

Lyons, C. A. (2003). *Teaching struggling readers: How to use brain-based research to maximize learning*. Portsmouth, NH: Heinemann.

Moss, B. (2005). Making a case and a place for effective content area literacy instruction in the elementary grades. *The Reading Teacher*, 59(1), 46–55.

Moss, B., & Young, T. A. (2010). *Creating lifelong readers through independent reading*. Newark, DE: International Reading Association.

Pinnell, G. S., & Fountas, I. C. (1998). *Word matters. Teaching phonics and spelling in the reading/writing classroom*. Portsmouth, NH: Heinemann.

Reading Recovery® Implementation:

Lyons, C. A., Pinnell, G. S., & DeFord, D. E. (1993). *Partners in learning. Teachers and children in Reading Recovery*. New York, NY: Teachers College Press.

Schmitt, M. C., Askew, B. J., Fountas, I. C., Lyons, C. A., & Pinnell, G. S. (2005). *Changing futures. The influence of Reading Recovery in the United States*. Worthington, OH: The Reading Recovery Council of North America.

Timperley, H., Wilson, A., Barrar, H., & Fung, I. (2007). Teacher professional learning and development: Best evidence synthesis iteration (BES). Available at www.readingrecovery.ac.nz/research

Watson, B., & Askew, B. (2009). *Boundless horizons: Marie Clay's search for the possible in children's literacy.* Portsmouth, NH: Heinemann.

Reading Recovery® Effectiveness:

Bates, C. C., D'Agostino, J. V., Gambrell, L., & Xu, M. (2016). Reading Recovery: Exploring the effects on first-graders' reading motivation and achievement. *Journal of Education for Students Placed at Risk, 21*(1), 47–59.

D'Agostino, J. V., & Harmey S. J. (2016). An international meta-analysis of Reading Recovery. *Journal of Education for Students Placed at Risk, 21*(1), 29–46.

International Data Evaluation Center. (2014–2015). *Reading Recovery statistical abstract for the U.S.* Columbus, OH: The Ohio State University. Available at www.idecweb.us

May, H., Sirinides, P., Gray, A., & Goldsworthy, H. (2016). *Reading Recovery: An evaluation of the four-year i3 scale-up.* Philadelphia, PA: Consortium for Policy Research in Education.

Schwartz, R. M. (2005a). Literacy learning of at-risk first-grade students in the Reading Recovery early intervention. *Journal of Educational Psychology, 97*(2), 257–267.

U.S. Department of Education, Institute of Education Sciences, What Works Clearinghouse. (2013, July). *Beginning Reading intervention report: Reading Recovery®.* Retrieved from http://ies.ed.gov/ncee/wwc/interventionreport.aspx?sid=420

References

Alvermann, D. E. (1991). The discussion web: A graphic aid for learning across the curriculum. *The Reading Teacher, 45*(2), 92–96.

Askew, B. J., Pinnell, G. S., & Scharer, P. L. (2014). *Promising literacy for every child: Reading Recovery® and a comprehensive literacy system.* Worthington, OH: The Reading Recovery Council of North America.

August, D., McCardle, P., & Shanahan, T. (2014). Developing literacy in English language learners: Findings from a review of the experimental research. *School Psychology Review, 43*(4), 490–498.

Ballantyne, A. (2009). Research origins: The historical context. In B. Watson & B. Askew (Eds.), *Boundless horizons: Marie Clay's search for the possible in children's literacy* (pp. 7–34). Portsmouth, NH: Heinemann.

Bear, D. R., Invernizzi, M. A., Johnston, F., & Templeton, S. (2015). *Words their way: Word study for phonics, vocabulary, and spelling.* Upper Saddle River, NJ: Pearson.

Beck, I. L., McKeown, M. G., & Kucan, L. (2002). *Bringing words to life.* New York, NY: Guilford Press.

Bennet, P. (2015). Supporting learning through instructional conversation. *The Journal of Reading Recovery, 15*(1), 35–44.

Berninger, V. W., Fuller, F., & Whittaker, D. (1996). A process model of writing across the life span. *Educational Psychology Review, 8*(3), 193–218.

Block, C. C., Parris, S. R., Reed, K. L., Whitely, C. S., & Cleveland, M. D. (2009). Instructional approaches which significantly increase reading comprehension. *Journal of Educational Psychology, 101*(2), 262–281.

Bloom, B., & Krathwohl, D. (1956). *Taxonomy of educational objectives: The classification of educational goals.* New York, NY: Longmans Green.

Brophy, J., & Alleman, J. (1991). Activities as instructional tools: A framework for analysis and evaluation. *Educational Researcher, 20*(4), 9–23.

Bruchac, J. (1999). *The trail of tears.* New York, NY: Random House.

Burningham, J. (1964). *John Burningham's ABC.* New York, NY: Crown.

Caldwell, J. S. (2008). *Comprehension assessment: A classroom guide.* New York, NY: Guilford Press.

California Department of Education (CDE). (2011). *California Common Core State Standards English language arts in history/social science, science, & technical subjects.* Retrieved from http://www.cde.ca.gov/re/cc/elaresources.asp

California Department of Education (CDE). (2012). *California English language development standards: Kindergarten through grade 12*. Retrieved from www.cde.ca.gov/sp/el/er/documents/eldstndspublication14.pdf

California Department of Education (CDE). (2014). *English language arts/English language development framework for California public schools*. Retrieved from www.cde.ca.gov/ci/rl/cf/elaeldfrmwrksbeadopted.asp

Calkins, L., Ehrenworth, M., & Lehman, C. (2012). *Pathways to the Common Core: Accelerating achievement*. Portsmouth, NH: Heinemann.

Cervetti, G. N., & Hiebert, E. H. (2015). The sixth pillar of reading instruction: Knowledge development. *The Reading Teacher, 68*(7), 548–551.

Clay, M. M. (1966). *Emergent reading behaviour* (Unpublished doctoral dissertation). University of Auckland, New Zealand.

Clay, M. M. (1971). The Polynesian language skills of Maori and Samoan school entrants. *International Journal of Psychology, 6*(2), 131–145.

Clay, M. M. (1975). *What did I write? Beginning writing behaviour.* Portsmouth, NH: Heinemann.

Clay, M. M. (1979). *Reading: The patterning of complex behaviour.* Auckland, New Zealand: Heinemann.

Clay, M. M. (1982). *Observing young readers. Selected papers.* Portsmouth, NH: Heinemann.

Clay, M. M. (1987). Learning to be learning disabled. *New Zealand Journal of Educational Studies, 22*(2), 155–173.

Clay, M. M. (1991a). *Becoming literate: The construction of inner control.* Portsmouth, NH: Heinemann.

Clay, M. M. (1991b). Child development. In J. Flood, J. M. Jensen, D. Lapp, & J. S. Squire (Eds.), *Handbook of research on teaching in the English Language Arts* (pp. 40–45). New York, NY: MacMillan.

Clay, M. M. (1993). *Reading Recovery: A guidebook for teachers in training.* Portsmouth, NH: Heinemann.

Clay, M. M. (2000a). *Running records for classroom teachers.* Portsmouth, NH: Heinemann.

Clay, M. M. (2000b). *Concepts about print: What have children learned about the way we print language?* Portsmouth, NH: Heinemann.

Clay, M. M. (2001). *Change over time in children's literacy development.* Portsmouth, NH: Heinemann.

Clay, M. M. (2005a). *Literacy lessons designed for individuals part one: Why? when? and how?* Portsmouth, NH: Heinemann.

Clay, M. M. (2005b). *Literacy lessons designed for individuals. Part two: Teaching procedures.* Portsmouth, NH: Heinemann.

Clay, M. M. (2013). *An observation survey of early literacy achievement* (3rd ed.). Portsmouth, NH: Heinemann.

Clay, M. M. (2014). *By different paths to common outcomes: Literacy learning and teaching* (2nd ed.). Auckland, New Zealand: The Marie Clay Literacy Trust.

Clay, M. M., Gill, M., Glynn, T., McNaughton, T., & Salmon, K. (1983). *Record of oral language and biks and gutches*. Auckland, New Zealand: Heinemann.

Concannon-Gibney, T., & Murphy, B. (2010). Reading practice in Irish primary classrooms: Too simple a view of reading? *Literacy, 44*(3), 122–130.

Connor, C. M., Morrison, F. J., Fishman, B., Giuliani, S., Luck, M., Underwood, P. S., . . . Schatschneider, C. (2011). Testing the impact of child characteristics x instruction interactions on third graders' reading comprehension by differentiating literacy instruction. *Reading Research Quarterly, 46*(3), 189–221.

Connor, C. M., Piasta, S. B., Glasney, S., Schatschneider, C., Crowe, E., Underwood, P., . . . Morrison, F. J. (2009). Individualizing student instruction precisely: Effects of child x instruction interactions on first graders' literacy development. *Child Development, 80*(1), 77–100.

Cooney, B. (1982). *Miss Rumphius.* New York, NY: Penguin.

D'Agostino, J. V., & Murphy. J. A. (2004). A meta-analysis of Reading Recovery in United States schools. *Educational Evaluation and Policy Analysis, 26*(1), 23–38.

Davies, N. (2009). *Extreme animals: The toughest creatures on earth*. New York, NY: Candlewick.

Day, J. P. (2001). How I became an exemplary teacher (Although I'm really still learning just like anyone else). In M. Pressley, R. L., Allington, R. Wharton-MacDonald, C. Collins-Block, & L. M. Morrow (Eds.), *Learning to read: Lessons from exemplary first-grade classrooms* (pp. 205–218). New York, NY: Guilford.

Denton, C. A. (2012). Response to intervention for reading difficulties in the primary grades: Some answers and lingering questions. *Journal of Learning Disabilities, 45*(3), 232–243.

Donovan, C. A., & Smolkin, L. B. (2011). Supporting informational writing in the elementary grades. *The Reading Teacher, 64*(6), 406–416.

Dorn, L., & Soffos, C. (2012). *Interventions that work: A comprehensive intervention model for preventing reading failure in grades K–3*. Boston, MA: Pearson Education.

Doyle, M. A. (2013). Marie M. Clay's theoretical perspective: A literacy processing theory. In D. E. Alvermann, N. J. Unrau, & R. B. Ruddell (Eds.), *Theoretical models and processes of reading* (pp. 636–656). Newark, DE: International Reading Association.

Duke, N. K., Pearson, P. D., Strachan, S. L, & Billman, A. K. (2011). Essential elements of fostering and teaching reading comprehension. In A. E. Farstrup & S. J. Samuels (Eds.), *What research has to say about reading instruction* (pp. 52–93). Newark, DE: International Reading Association.

Dyson, A. H. (1997). *Writing superheroes: Contemporary childhood, popular culture, and classroom literacy*. New York, NY: Teachers College Press.

Echevarria, J., Frey, N., & Fisher (2015, March). What it takes for English learners to succeed. *Educational Leadership, 72*(6), 22–26.

Fearn, L., & Farnan, N. (2001). *Interactions: Teaching writing and the language arts.* Boston, MA: Houghton Mifflin.

Fisher, D., Frey, N., & Rothenberg, C. (2008). *Content area conversations: How to plan discussion-based lessons for diverse language learners.* Alexandria, VA: Association for Supervision and Curriculum Development.

Ford, M. P., & Opitz, M. F. (2010). Moving from many and most to every and all: Research-based practices for moving all readers forward. *Illinois Reading Council Journal, 38*(4), 3–13.

Fountas, I. C., & Pinnell, G. S. (1996). *Guided reading. Good first teaching for all children.* Portsmouth, NH: Heinemann.

Fountas, I. C., & Pinnell, G. S. (2012a). Guided reading: The romance and the reality. *Reading Teacher, 66*(4), 268–284.

Fountas, I. C., & Pinnell, G. S. (2012b). *Fountas & Pinnell prompting guide. Part 2 for comprehension: Thinking, talking, and writing.* Portsmouth, NH: Heinemann.

Fountas, I. C., & Pinnell, G. S. (2013). *The Fountas and Pinnell leveled book list, K–8.* Portsmouth, NH: Heinemann.

Fountas, I. C., & Pinnell, G. S. (2014, July). *The critical role of text complexity in teaching children to read.* Retrieved from www.heinemann.com/fountasandpinnell/supportingMaterials/fountasAndPinnellTextComplexityWhitePaper.pdf

Gaffney, J. S., & Askew, B. J. (1999). Marie M. Clay. In J. S. Gaffney & B. J. Askew (Eds.), *Stirring the waters: The influence of Marie Clay* (pp. ix–xiii). Portsmouth, NH: Heinemann.

Ganske, K., & Jocius, R. (2013). Small-group word study: Instructional conversations or mini-interrogations? *Language Arts, 91*(1), 23–40.

Gersten, R., Baker, S. K., Shanahan, T., Linan-Thompson, S., Collins, P., & Scarcella, R. (2007). *Effective literacy and English language instruction for English learners in the elementary grades: A practice guide* (NCEE 2007-4011). Washington, DC: National Center for Education Evaluation and Regional Assistance, Institute of Education Sciences, U.S. Department of Education. Retrieved from ies.ed.gov/ncee/wwc/publications/practiceguides

Gibson, S. A. (2008). An effective framework for primary-grade guided writing lessons. *The Reading Teacher, 62*(4), 324–334.

Gibson, S. A., & Ross, P. (2016). Teachers' professional noticing, *Theory Into Practice, 55*(3), 180–188.

Giles, J. (1997). *Just one guinea pig.* Crystal Lake, IL: Rigby.

Glenday, C. (2015). *Guinness world records 2015.* New York, NY: Bantam Books.

Gough, P. B., & Tunmer, W. E. (1986). Decoding, reading, and reading disability. *Remedial and Special Education, 7*, 6–10.

Graham, S., Bollinger, A., Olson, C. B., D'Aoust, D., MacArthur, C., McCutchen, D., & Olinghouse, N. (2012). *Teaching elementary school students to be effective writers: A practice guide* (NCEE 2012-4058). Washington, DC: National Center for Education Evaluation and Regional Assistance, Institute of Education Sciences, U.S. Department of Education. Retrieved from ies. ed.gov/ncee/wwc/publications_reviews.aspx#pubsearch

Hiebert, E. H., & Van Sluys, K. (2014). Examining three assumptions about text complexity: Standard 10 of the Common Core State Standards. In K. S. Goodman, R. C. Calfee, & Y. M. Goodman (Eds.), *Whose knowledge counts in government literacy policies? Why expertise matters* (pp. 144–160). New York, NY: Routledge.

Hilden, K., & Jones, J. (2012). A literacy spring cleaning: Sweeping round robin reading out of your classroom. *Reading Today, 29*(5), 23-24.

Hirsch, E. D. (2003). Reading comprehension requires knowledge of words and the world. *American Educator, 27*(1), 10–29, 44–45.

Hoban, T. (1987). *26 letters and 99 cents.* New York, NY: Greenwillow Press.

Hoge, R. D., & Coladarci, T. (1989). Teacher-based judgments of academic achievement: A review of literature. *Review of Educational Research, 59*(3), 297–313.

Holdaway, D. (1984). *The foundations of literacy.* Portsmouth, NH: Heinemann.

Houck, B. D., & Ross, K. (2012). Dismantling the myth of learning to read and reading to learn. *ASCD Express, 7*(11).

Hurd, E. T. (2000). *Starfish.* New York, NY: HarperCollins.

International Data Evaluation Center. (2014–2015). *Reading Recovery national summary report for the United States.* Columbus, OH: The Ohio State University.

International Literacy Association. (2016). *Dyslexia* [Research advisory]. Newark, DE: Author.

Irwin, M. M. (1948). *Teaching of reading to special class children.* (Unpublished master's thesis). Wellington: Victoria College, The University of New Zealand.

Jacobs, V. R., Lamb, L. L. C., Philipp, R. A., & Schappelle, B. P. (2011). Deciding how to respond on the basis of children's understandings. In M. G. Sherin, V. R. Jacobs, & R. A. Philipp (Eds.), *Mathematics teacher noticing. Seeing through teachers' eyes* (pp. 97–116). New York, NY: Routledge.

Jenkins, S. (2005). *I see a kookaburra: Animal habitats around the world.* New York, NY: Houghton Mifflin Harcourt.

Jenkins, S. (2006). *Almost gone: The world's rarest animals* (Let's read and find out science 2). New York, NY: HarperCollins.

Johnson, E. S., Jenkins, J. R., & Jewell, M. (2005). Analyzing components of reading on performance assessments: An expanded simple view. *Reading Psychology, 26*, 267–283.

Johnston, P. (2003). Assessment conversations. *The Reading Teacher, 57*(1), 90–92.

Johnston, P. H., & Allington, R. (1991). Remediation. In R. Barr, M. Kamil, P. Mosenthal, & P. D. Pearson (Eds.), *Handbook of reading research* (pp. 984–1012). New York, NY: Longman.

Jones, C. D., & Reutzel, D. R. (2012). Enhanced alphabet knowledge instruction: Exploring a change of frequency, focus, and distributed cycles of review. *Reading Psychology, 33*(5), 448–464.

Joshi, R. M., & Aaron, P. G. (2000). The component model of reading: Simple view of reading made a little more complex. *Reading Psychology, 21*, 85–97.

Kaye, E. L. (2006). Second graders' reading behaviors: A study of variety, complexity, and change. *Literacy Teaching and Learning, 10*(2), 51–75.

Kaye, E. L., & Lose, M. K. (2015). More than ABCs: Letter knowledge and the development of a literacy processing system. *The Journal of Reading Recovery, 15*(1), 5–20.

Kelly, P. R. (1995). Round robin reading: Considering alternative instructional practices that make more sense. *Reading Horizons, 36*(2), 99–115.

Kirby, J., & Savage, R. S. (2008). Can the simple view deal with the complexities of reading? *Literacy, 42*(2), 75–82.

Kucer, S. B. (2014). *Dimensions of literacy: A conceptual base for teaching reading and writing in school settings.* New York, NY: Routledge.

Kuhn, M. R., & Schwanenflugel, P. J. (2006). All oral reading practice is not equal or how can I integrate fluency into my classroom? *Literacy Teaching and Learning: An International Journal of Early Reading and Writing, 11*(1), 1–20.

Kuhn, M. R., Schwanenflugel, P. J., Morris, R. D., Morrow, L. M., Woo, D. G., Meisinger, E. B., . . . Stahl, S. (2006). Teaching children to become fluent and automatic readers. *Journal of Literacy Research, 38*(4), 357–387.

Lapp, D., Moss, B., Grant, M., & Johnson, K. (2015). *A close look at close reading: Teaching students to analyze complex texts, Grades K–5.* Alexandria, VA: Association for Supervision and Curriculum Development.

Lobel, A., (1972). *Frog and toad together.* New York, NY: HarperCollins.

Malcolm, M. (1983). *I can read.* Wellington, New Zealand: Learning Media Limited.

Manyak, P. C., Von Gunten, H., Autenrieth, D., Gillis, C., Mastre-O'Farrell, J., Irvine-McDermott, E., Baumann, J. F., & Blachowicz, C. (2014). Four practical principles for enhancing vocabulary instruction. *The Reading Teacher, 68*(1), 13–23.

May, H., Sirinides, P., Gray, A., & Goldsworthy, H. (2016). *Reading Recovery: An evaluation of the four-year i3 scale-up.* Philadelphia, PA: Consortium for Policy Research in Education.

McCloskey, R. (1952). *One morning in Maine.* New York, NY: Penguin Group.

McGee, L. M., Kim, H., Nelson, K. S., & Fried, M. D. (2015). Change over time in first graders' strategic use of information at point of difficulty in reading. *Reading Research Quarterly, 50*(3), 263–291.

McKay, R., & Teale, W. H. (2015). *No more teaching a letter a week.* Portsmouth, NH: Heinemann.

McLaughlin, M. (2013). Read-alouds and recreational reading always! Round-robin reading never! *Reading Today, 31*(1), 2–3.

McNamara, D. S., & Kintsch, W. (1996). Learning from texts: Effects of prior knowledge and text coherence. *Discourse Processes, 22*(3), 247–288.

McNaughton, S. (2014). Classroom instruction. The influences of Marie Clay. *The Reading Teacher, 69*(2), 88–92.

Miller, A. C., & Keenan, J. M. (2009). How word decoding skill impacts text memory: The centrality deficit and how domain knowledge can compensate. *Annals of Dyslexia, 59*(2), 99–113.

Morrow, L. M. (1996). Story retelling: A discussion strategy to develop and assess comprehension. In L. B. Gambrell & Almasi, J. F. (Eds.), *Lively discussions! Fostering engaged reading* (pp. 265–285). Newark, DE: International Reading Association.

Morrow, L. M., Tracey, D. H., Woo, D. G., & Pressley, M. (1999). Characteristics of exemplary first-grade literacy instruction. *The Reading Teacher, 53*(5), 462–176.

Moss, B. (2005). Making a case and a place for effective content area literacy instruction in the elementary grades. *The Reading Teacher, 59*(1), 46–55.

Moss, B., & Young, T. A. (2010). *Creating lifelong readers through independent reading.* Newark, DE: International Reading Association.

National Council of Teachers of English. (2008). *English language learners: Supplemental resources for NCTE's policy research brief.* Urbana, IL: Author. Retrieved from www.ncte.org/library/NCTEFiles/Resources/PolicyResearch/ ELLResearchBrief.pdf

National Governors Association Center for Best Practice & Council of Chief State School Officers. (NGACBP & CCSSO). (2010). *Common Core State Standards for English language arts & literacy in history/social studies, science, and technical subjects.* Washington, DC: Authors.

National Institute of Child Health and Human Development. (2000). *Teaching children to read: An evidence-based assessment of the scientific research literature on reading and its implications for reading instruction* (NIH Publication No. 00-4769) [Report of the National Reading Panel]. Washington, DC: U.S. Government Printing Office.

Neuman, S. B. (2001). The role of knowledge in early literacy. *Reading Research Quarterly, 36*(4), 468–475.

Neuman, S. B., Kaefer, T., & Pinkhorn, A. (2014). Building background knowledge. *The Reading Teacher, 68*(2), 145–148.

Newmann, F. M., Bryk, A. S., & Nagaoka, J. K. (2001). *Authentic intellectual work and standardized tests: Conflict or coexistence?* Chicago, IL: Consortium on Chicago School Research.

O'Leary, S. (2009). Teaching essential vocabulary to English language learners. In C. Rodriguez-Eagle (Ed.), *Achieving success with English language learners: Insights, assessment, instruction* (pp. 125–142). Worthington, OH: Reading Recovery Council of North America.

Osborn, A. F. (1953). *Applied imagination: Principles and procedures of creative problem solving*. New York, NY: Charles Scribner's Sons.

Partnership for 21st Century Skills. (2013). Framework for 21st century learning. Retrieved from

Pearson, P. D., Hansen, J., & Gordon, C. (1979). The effect of background knowledge on young children's comprehension of explicit and implicit information. *Journal of Reading Behavior, 11,* 201–209.

Pearson, P. D., Valencia, S. W., & Wixson, K. (2014). Complicating the world of reading assessment: Toward better assessments for better teaching. *Theory into Practice, 53,* 236–246.

Polacco, P. (1996). *The keeping quilt*. New York, NY: Simon & Schuster

Pressley, M., Allington, R. L., Wharton-MacDonald, R., Collins-Block, C., & Morrow, L. M. (2001). *Learning to read: Lessons from exemplary first-grade classrooms*. New York, NY: Guilford.

Priebe, S. J., Keenan, J. M, & Miller, A. C. (2012). How prior knowledge affects word identification and comprehension. *Reading and Writing, 25*(1), 131–149.

RAND Reading Study Group. (2002). *Reading for understanding: Toward an R&D program in reading comprehension*. Santa Monica, CA: RAND.

Rapp, D. N, van den Broek, P., McMaster, K. L, Kendeou, P., & Espin, C. A. (2007). Higher-order comprehension processes in struggling readers: A perspective for research and intervention. *Scientific Studies of Reading, 11*(4), 289–312.

Rasinski, R. V., Reutzel, D. R., Chard, D., & Linan-Thompson, S. (2011). Reading fluency. In M. L. Kamil, P. D. Pearson, E. B. Moje, & P. P. Afflerbach (Eds.), *Handbook of reading research, Vol. IV.* New York, NY: Routledge.

Robb, L. (2002). The myth of learn to read/read to learn. *Instructor, 11*(8), 23–25.

Robertson, D. A., Dougherty, S., Ford-Connors, E., & Paratore, J. R. (2014). Re-envisioning instruction. *The Reading Teacher, 67*(7), 547–559.

Ross, P., & Gibson, S. A. (2010). Exploring a conceptual framework for expert noticing during literacy instruction. *Literacy Research and Instruction, 49*(2), 175–193.

Schmitt, M. C., Askew, B. J., Fountas, I. C., Lyons, C. A., & Pinnell, G. S. (2005). *Changing futures: The influence of Reading Recovery in the United States*. Worthington, OH: The Reading Recovery Council of North America.

Schwartz, R. M. (2005a). Literacy learning of at-risk first-grade students in the Reading Recovery early intervention. *Journal of Educational Psychology, 97*(2), 257–267.

Schwartz, R. M. (2005b). Decisions, decisions: Responding to primary students during guided reading. *The Reading Teacher, 58*(5), 436–443.

Schwartz, R. M. (2015). Why not sound it out? *The Journal of Reading Recovery, 14*(2), 39–46.

Searfoss, L. (1975). Radio reading. *The Reading Teacher, 29*(3), 295–296.

Shanahan, T., Callison, K., Carriere, C., Duke, N. K., Pearson, P. D., Schatschneider, C., & Torgesen, J. (2010). *Improving reading comprehension in kindergarten through 3rd grade: A practice guide* (NCEE 2010-4038). Washington, DC: National Center for Education Evaluation and Regional Assistance, Institute of Education Sciences, U.S. Department of Education. Retrieved from whatworks. ed.gov/publications/practiceguides

Siamon, S. (1992). *I like to eat.* Carlsbad, CA: Dominie Press.

Slowik, H. Y., & Brynelson, N. (2015). *Executive summary: English language arts/English language development framework for California public schools: Kindergarten through grade twelve.* Sacramento, CA: Consortium for the Implementation of the Common Core State Standards.

Sloyer, S. (1982). *Readers theatre: Story dramatization in the classroom.* Urbana, IL: National Council of Teachers of English.

Snow, C. E., Burns, M. S., & Griffin, P. (Eds.). (1998). *Preventing reading difficulties.* Washington, DC: National Academy Press.

Snyder, I. (2003). *Milk to ice cream.* New York, NY: Children's Press.

Sparks, S. D. (2016, March). i3 grants: Findings from the first round. *Education Week.* Retrieved from www.edweek.org/ew/section/multimedia/i3-grants-findings-from-the-first-round.html?cmp=eml-enl-eu-news1

Stahl, S. A., & Heubach, K. (2005). Fluency-oriented reading instruction. *Journal of Literacy Research, 37*(1), 25–60.

Stauffer, R. G. (1970). *The language-experience approach to the teaching of reading.* New York, NY: Harper & Row.

Sulzby, E. (1992). Research directions: Transitions from emergent to conventional writing. *Language Arts, 69*(4), 290.

Taba, H. (1967). *Teachers handbook for elementary social studies.* Reading, MA: Addison-Wesley.

Taft, M. L., & Leslie, L. (1985). The effects of prior knowledge and oral reading accuracy on miscues and comprehension. *Journal of Reading Behavior, 17,* 163–179.

Taylor, B. M., Pearson, P. D., Clark, K., & Walpole, S. (2000). Effective schools and accomplished teachers: Lessons about primary-grade reading instruction in low-income schools. *The Elementary School Journal, 101*(2), 121–165.

Tharp, R. (1982). The effective instruction of comprehension: Results and description of the Kamehameha Early Education Program. *Reading Research Quarterly, 17*(4), 503–527.

Thomson, S. L. (2006). *Amazing whales.* New York, NY: HarperCollins.

Tiu, R. D., Thompson, L. A., & Lewis, B. A. (2003). The role of IQ in a component model of reading. *Journal of Learning Disabilities, 36,* 424–436.

Topping, K. (1987). Paired reading: A powerful technique for parent use. *The Reading Teacher, 40*(7), 608–614.

U.S. Department of Education, Institute of Education Sciences, What Works Clearinghouse (2013, July). *Beginning reading intervention report: Reading Recovery®.* Retrieved from http://ies.ed.gov/ncee/wwc/interventionreport. aspx?sid=420

Vellutino, F. R. (2010). "Learning to be learning disabled": Marie Clay's seminal contribution to the response to intervention approach to identifying specific reading disability. *The Journal of Reading Recovery, 10*(1), 5–23.

Vellutino, F. R., Fletcher, J. M., Snowling, M. J., & Scanlon, D. M. (2004). Specific reading disability (dyslexia): What have we learned in the past four decades? *Journal of Child Psychology & Psychiatry, 45*(1), 2–40.

Vellutino, F. R., Scanlon, D. M., Sipay, E. R., Small, S. G., Pratt, A., Chen, R., & Denckla, M. B. (1996). Cognitive profiles of difficult-to-remediate and readily remediated poor readers: Early intervention as a vehicle for distinguishing between cognitive and experiential deficits as basic causes of specific reading disability. *Journal of Educational Psychology, 88*(4), 601–638.

Vellutino, F. R., Scanlon, D. M., Zhang, H., & Schatschneider, C. (2008). Using response to kindergarten and first grade intervention to identify children at-risk for long-term reading difficulties. *Reading & Writing, 21*(4), 437–480.

Watson, B. (1999). Creating independent learners. In J. S. Gaffney & B. J. Askew (Eds.), *Stirring the waters. The influence of Marie Clay* (pp. 47–74). Portsmouth, NH: Heinemann.

Watson, B., & Askew, B. (Eds.). (2009). *Boundless horizons. Marie Clay's search for the possible in children's literacy.* Portsmouth, NH: Heinemann.

Watts-Taffe, S., Laster, B. P., Broach, L., Marinak, B., Connor, C. M., & Walker-Dalhouse, D. (2013). Differentiated instruction: Making informed teacher decisions. *The Reading Teacher, 66*(4), 303–314.

Wharton-McDonald, R., Pressley, M., & Hampston, J. M. (1998). Literacy instruction in nine first-grade classrooms: Teacher characteristics and student achievement. *Elementary School Journal, 99*, 101–128.

Williams, J. L. (2013). Common ground: Reading Recovery and the Common Core State Standards. *The Journal of Reading Recovery, 12*(2), 15–25.

Wold, J. (2002). Teachers' reflections and meaningful actions. In E. M. Rodgers & G. S. Pinnell (Eds.), *Learning from teaching in literacy education: New perspectives on professional development* (pp. 79–92). Portsmouth, NH: Heinemann.

Wood, D., Bruner, J. S., & Ross, G. (1976). The role of tutoring in problem solving. *Journal of Child Psychology and Psychiatry, 17*, 89–100.

Wright, W. E. (2016). Let them talk! To promote ELLs' literacy growth and content-area achievement, don't neglect their English oral-language skills. *Educational Leadership, 78*(5), 24–29.

Yancey, K. B. (2009). *Writing in the 21st century. A report from the National Council of Teachers of English.* Urbana, IL: National Council of Teachers of English. Retrieved from www.ncte.org/library/NCTEFiles/Press/Yancey_final.pdf

Index

Aaron, P. G., 7

ABC books, 42

Accuracy scores, 1–2, 11, 29, 38, 46, 102–103, 105–106, 108, 111

Activities
  constructive learners and, 25–26
  Paired Reading activity, 24
  paired research, 75, 76–77
  problem-solving. *See* Problem-solving activities
  strategic. *See* Strategic activity
  in units of study, 69–71, 73–75
  work-time activities or centers, 25–26

Activity centers, 25–26

Alice (teacher), 71–75

Alleman, J., 69

Allington, R. L., 16, 19, 20, 33, 45

Almost Gone! (Jenkins), 74, 75

Alphabet books, 42

Alvermann, D. E., 51, 58–59

Amazing Whales! (Thomson), 74

Analytic assessment, 92, 93

Andrew (teacher), 33–35, 38, 40–41, 43–45

Animal Habitats (National Geographic Windows on Literacy Language, Literacy and Vocabulary), 74

Anna (student), 27–29

Application questions, 57

Art, integrating writing instruction in, 93–94

Askew, B. J., 3, 16, 121–122

Assessment
  analytic, 92, 93
  formative, 48, 71
  running record, 27–29, 33, 44–45, 91–92, 104–105
  summative, 72

Audio recordings, 105

August, D., 109

Autenrieth, D., 110

Background knowledge, 64

Baker, S. K., 108, 110

Ballantyne, A., 3

Basal reading programs, 52, 66, 100, 106–107

Baumann, J. F., 110

Bear, D. R., 29

Beck, I. L., 109–110

Becoming Literate (Clay, 1991a), 9, 10, 16, 21, 23–24, 32, 46, 49, 51, 59, 61–62, 100, 102, 105

Bennet, P., 20, 58

Berninger, V. W., 90

Billman, A. K., 65

Blachowicz, C., 110

Block, C. C., 18

Bloom, B., 56

Bollinger, A., 92–93

Brainstorming, 90

Broach, L., 20

Brophy, J., 69

Bruchac, J., 97–100, 102–104, 109–110

Bruner, J. S., 48

Bryk, A. S., 26
Brynelson, N., 32
Burningham, John, 42
Burns, M. S., 51
*By Different Paths to Common
    Outcomes* (Clay, 2014), 2, 8,
    14–16, 17, 25–27, 32, 36, 41, 48,
    56, 57–58, 60, 63, 64, 78, 80,
    82–83, 86, 87, 89, 90–91, 95, 109,
    113–114

Caldwell, J. S., 56
California Department of Education
    (CDE), 9, 18, 32, 33, 95, 97–98,
    104
Calkins, L., 89, 104
Callison, K., 50
Carriere, C., 50
Cervetti, G. N., 63
*Change Over Time in Children's
    Literacy Development* (Clay, 2001),
    1, 5, 7–8, 10–11, 14, 16, 17, 18,
    33, 35–36, 41, 49, 50, 51, 61–62,
    63, 64, 80, 83, 85–86, 89, 94, 96,
    99, 100, 109, 111–112
Chard, D., 106
Chen, R., 17
"Child Development" (Clay, 1991b),
    86, 98
Choice, in writing informational
    texts, 90–91
Choral reading, 70, 105, 107
Clark, K., 51
Classroom schedules
    dedicated time for writing in,
        92–94
    in differentiated classroom
        instruction, 18, 20, 21, 117
Clay, Marie M. *See also* Clay, Marie
    M. works; Complex view of
    literacy processing; Literacy
    processing theory; Reading
    RecoveryRX
    basis of research and theory

development, 1–3
comprehension as priority in
    reading, 10, 59, 63
concepts about print, 32, 36–45
differentiated classroom
    instruction and, 1, 5, 11,
    14–31
knowledge categories, 61–63
planning comprehensive literacy
    program, 113–114, 116
reading, defined, 61
research and theory development
    overview, 1–3
strategic activity, defined, 5, 49
systematic observation of literacy
    behaviors. *See* Systematic
    observation
teaching as adaptive expertise, 44
teaching foundational skills,
    32–45
writing informational texts, 69–
    70, 79–95
Clay, Marie M. works
Becoming Literate (1991a), 9, 10,
    16, 21, 23–24, 32, 46, 49, 51,
    59, 61–62, 100, 102, 105
*By Different Paths to Common
    Outcomes* (2014), 2, 8, 14–16,
    17, 25–27, 32, 36, 41, 48,
    56, 57–58, 60, 63, 64, 78, 80,
    82–83, 86, 87, 89, 90–91, 95,
    109, 113–114
*Change Over Time in Children's
    Literacy Development* (2001),
    1, 5, 7–8, 10–11, 14, 16, 17,
    18, 33, 35–36, 41, 49, 50, 51,
    61–62, 63, 64, 80, 83, 85–86,
    89, 94, 96, 99, 100, 109,
    111–112
"Child Development" (1991b),
    86, 98
Concepts About Print (2000b), 45
Emergent Reading Behaviour
    (1966), 3, 6

"Learning to be Learning
Disabled" (1987), 17
*Literacy Lessons Designed for
Individuals Part One* (2005a),
2, 7, 33, 35–36, 61–63, 87,
104, 105
*Literacy Lessons Designed for
Individuals Part Two* (2005b),
1, 2, 5, 7–9, 10, 17, 20, 22,
28, 32, 34, 36–39, 41–43, 48,
51, 57, 96, 100, 102, 104,
105, 111
*Observation Survey of Early
Literacy Achievement, An*
(2013), 26, 27, 29, 32, 91,
104–105, 116
Observing Young Readers (1982),
3, 6, 32, 51
"Polynesian Language Skills of
Maori and Samoan School
Entrants, The" (1971), 3
Reading (1979), 2
Reading Recovery (1993), 2, 3
*Running Records for Classroom
Teachers* (2000a), 27, 29, 31,
104–105, 116
"What Did I Write?" (1975), 7
Cleveland, M. D., 18
Close Look at Close Reading, A
(Lapp et al.), 78
Close reading
deep knowledge and, 65
in planning units of study, 69, 77,
78
Cognates, 111
Coladarci, T., 120
Collaboration
among teachers and education
professionals, 1, 67, 80–85,
119–121
of struggling readers and writers,
24
of students in research projects,
75–77
of students in writing projects, 9
Collins-Block, C., 16, 19, 20, 33, 45
Collins, P., 108, 110
Commercial reading programs, 14,
15–16, 17
Common Core State Standards
(CCSS), 9, 32, 61, 62, 67, 71–72,
90, 94, 95. *See also* California
Department of Education (CDE)
Complex text, 100
Complex view of literacy processing
fast past of learning, 97–100,
106–111
fluency-oriented reading
instruction (FORI), 106–108
multiple aspects of literacy tasks
in, 7–8, 26
rigor in K-2 classroom literacy
instruction, 98–106
simple view versus, 7
text complexity levels, 100–106
vocabulary instruction for English
language learners, 108–111
Comprehension
design and implementation of
instruction in, 59–60
foundational skills instruction
and, 50–51
integrating with decoding
instruction, 47–49, 50
in knowledge-building process,
63, 64
as priority in reading, 10, 59, 63
strategic activities for, 50–59
teaching for meaning and, 50–59
Concannon-Gibney, T., 7
Concepts about print, 36–45
directionality in English, 36, 38,
39
letter/word knowledge, 32, 34, 35,
36–37, 38–44
nature of, 36–37
prompting for children's use of,
38, 42–44

Concepts about print (*continued*)
   punctuation, 39
   shared reading and, 37–38, 39
   spaces or word boundaries, 36, 39
   teaching, 37–38
Concepts About Print (Clay, 2000b),
   45
Connor, C. M., 18, 20
Consortium for Policy Research in
   Education, 114
Constructive learners, 25–26
Content knowledge, 63, 64
   integrating writing instruction in,
      93–94
   in planning units of study, 67, 68
Content Workshop, 93
Continuous text, 5, 9–10, 34, 36, 61,
   85, 91, 114
Cooney, B., 52–54
Council of Chief State School
   Officers (CCSSO), 9, 10, 26, 62,
   90, 100
Couplet writing, 84–85
Crabtree Publishing, 73, 74
Crowe, E., 20

D'Agostino, J. V., 2
D'Aoust, D., 92–93
Davies, Nicola, 65
Day, J. P., 30, 114, 121, 122
"Decisions, Decisions" (Schwartz),
   31
Decoding, integrating with
   comprehension instruction, 47–
   49, 50
Deep knowledge, 64, 65
Demonstration lessons, 73
Denckla, M. B., 17
Denton, C. A., 16
Dialogue journals, 69
Differentiated classroom instruction,
   14–31
   classroom schedules in, 18, 20,
      21, 117

commercial reading programs
   versus, 14, 15–16, 17
   described, 14
   for foundational skills, 35
   grouping for instruction, 18–26
   implementing, 11, 14–15, 18–26
   importance of, 1, 5, 14, 15–18
   principles of, 17–18
   starting points for teachers, 30
   systematic observation of literacy
      behaviors as basis. *See*
      Systematic observation
Discussion Web, The (Alvermann), 51,
   58–59
Document viewers, 54, 90, 110
Domain knowledge, 64
Donovan, C. A., 84
Dorn, L., 93
Doyle, M. A., 6, 7, 32, 61, 62, 89, 99
Drafting, 87, 94
Duke, N. K., 50, 65
Dyson, A. H., 90

Earth's Endangered Creatures, 74
Easy text, 106
Echevarria, J., 104
Echo reading, 105, 107
"Effective Framework for Primary-
   Grade Guided Writing Instruction,
   An" (Gibson), 95
Ehrenworth, M., 89, 104
Elian (student), 4–7
Emergent Reading Behaviour (Clay,
   1966), 3, 6
Engage NY, 73, 74
English language learners (ELLs), 17
   in complex view of literacy
      processing, 97–100
   foundational skills development,
      33
   in heterogeneous groups, 24
   vocabulary development, 108–111
   writing informational texts, 87
Environmental print, 37

Espin, C. A., 64
Essential questions, in planning units of study, 67, 68
Exemplary teachers, 16, 19, 20, 30, 33, 51, 114, 119
Experience-Text Relationship (Tharp), 57–58
Extreme Animals (Davies), 65

Familiar text, 105
Farnan, N., 88, 91, 92
Fearn, L., 88, 91, 92
Fisher, D., 91, 104
Fishman, B., 18, 20
Fletcher, J. M., 17
Florida Panthers (National Wildlife Foundation), 74, 76
Fluency, 32
Fluency-oriented reading instruction (FORI), 106–108
Ford, M. P., 26
Formative assessment
 partner talk in, 48
 units of study, 71
Foundational skills, 32–45
 Andrew (teacher) and, 33–35, 38, 40–41, 43–45
 complex learning and, 32
 comprehension instruction and, 50–51
 concepts about print, 32, 36–45
 in context, 35–36
 defining, 32
 differentiated instruction for, 35
 integrated opportunities to learn, 33–36
 letter/word knowledge, 32, 33, 34, 35, 36–37, 38–44
 links between language sounds and text, 32, 33, 34–35, 36
 teaching in isolation, 34–35
Fountas, I. C., 16, 20–21, 57, 101–104
Frey, N., 91, 104

Fried, M. D., 44
Frog and Toad Together (Lobel), 19
Frustration level text, 100–102
Fuller, F., 90

Gaffney, J. S., 3
Ganske, K., 108, 109
Gersten, R., 108, 110
Gibson, S. A., 14, 29, 88, 95, 118, 119
Giles, J., 47–48, 58–59, 101
Gillis, C., 110
Giuliani, S., 18, 20
Glasney, S., 20
Glenday, C., 24
Goldsworthy, H., 1, 2, 11, 114
Gordon, C., 64
Gough, P. B., 7
Grace (teacher), 80–85, 87, 91–94
Graham, S., 92–93
Grant, M., 78
Graphic organizers, 54, 55–56, 76–77, 80–83
Gray, A., 1, 2, 11, 114
Griffin, P., 51
Grouping for instruction. *See* Small-group instruction; Whole-class instruction
Guided reading
 deep knowledge and, 65
 homogeneous groups in, 20–21
 in planning units of study, 69, 73
Guided retelling, 54–55

Hampston, J. M., 51
Hansen, J., 64
Heterogeneous groups, 24
Heubach, K., 106–108
Hiebert, E. H., 63, 100
High-frequency words, 5, 7
Hilden, K., 22
Hirsch, E. D., 63–64
Hoban, T., 42
Hoge, R. D., 120

Holdaway, D., 37
Homogeneous groups, 20–22
Houck, B. D., 50
Howard (student), 27, 28
"How I Became an Exemplary
    Teacher" (Day), 122
Hurd, E. T., 73, 74

I Can Read (Malcolm), 50
I Like to Eat (Siamon), 36
Independent reading, 21, 22, 25, 29,
    36, 38, 47, 49, 69, 86, 98, 104,
    105, 106, 111
Independent writing, 79, 81–83, 86,
    94, 95
Inferential questions, 56–57
Informational texts, 61–95
    building knowledge through,
        64–65
    incorporating in the classroom,
        61–62
    information needed to become
        literate, 61–62
    types of, 61
    in units of study, 66–77
    writing by students. *See* Writing
        informational texts
Instructional density, 19–20
Instructional level text, 102–105
Instructional scaffolding, 48, 50, 59,
    75, 77, 78, 86, 117
Interactive read-aloud and teacher
    questioning, 51–54
Interest-based groups, 24
International Data Evaluation Center,
    2
International Literacy Association,
    17, 37
Introducing Habitats series, 74
Invernizzi, M. A., 29
Irvine-McDermott, E., 110
Irwin, M. M., 3
I See a Kookaburra (Jenkins), 73, 74

Jacobs, V. R., 118
Jenkins, J. R., 7
Jenkins, S., 73–75
Jewell, M., 7
Jocius, R., 108, 109
John Burningham's ABC
    (Burningham), 42
Johnson, E. S., 7
Johnson, K., 78
Johnston, F., 29
Johnston, P. H., 16, 115
Jones, C. D., 39, 40
Jones, J., 22
Joshi, R. M., 7
Journals, dialogue, 69
Julie (teacher), 47–48
Just One Guinea Pig (Giles), 47–48,
    58–59, 101

Kaefer, T., 63
Karen (student), 4–6
Kaye, E. L., 38, 98
Keenan, J. M., 63, 64
Keeping Quilt, The (Polacco), 49
Kelly, P. R., 22
Kendeou, P., 64
Kids' Planet, 74
Kim, H., 44
Kintsch, W., 64
Kirby, J., 7
Knowledge-building, 61–95
    comparing and contrasting
        information formats, 65
    comprehension in, 63, 64
    content knowledge and, 63, 64
    knowledge categories, 61–63
    knowledge in literacy
        development, 63–64
    as prewriting process, 90
    prior knowledge and, 63
    texts in, 64–65
    types of knowledge, 62–64
    units of study in, 66–77
Krathwohl, D., 56

Kucan, L., 109–110
Kucer, S. B., 49–51
Kuhn, M. R., 106

Lamb, L. L. C., 118
Language Experience Approach
   (Stauffer), 69
Language Workshop, 93
Lapp, D., 78
Laster, B. P., 20
Leadership. *See* Teacher leadership
Learning disability, students with,
   17, 37
Learning logs, 69
"Learning to be Learning Disabled"
   (Clay, 1987), 17
Lehman, C., 89, 104
Leslie, L., 64
Letter/word knowledge, 32
   alphabet books, 42
   components of, 40
   differentiated instruction, 35
   fast responses to visual
      information, 34–35
   teaching for comprehensive,
      39–44
   writing letters, 41–42
Leveled books, 73
Lewis, B. A., 7
Linan-Thompson, S., 106, 108, 110
Listening activities, in units of study,
   70
List Group Label activity (Taba), 90
*Literacy Lessons Designed for
   Individuals Part One* (Clay, 2005a),
   2, 7, 33, 35–36, 61–63, 87, 104,
   105
*Literacy Lessons Designed for
   Individuals Part Two* (Clay, 2005b),
   1, 2, 5, 7–9, 10, 17, 20, 22, 28, 32,
   34, 36–39, 41–43, 48, 51, 57, 96,
   100, 102, 104, 105, 111
Literacy processing theory, 6–11
   all language knowledge sources

   in, 62
basis of Clay's research and theory
   development, 3
comparison with California
   Department of Education
   (CDE), 95
complex view. *See* Complex view
   of literacy processing
constructing ideas into written
   language, 85–89
continuous text role in, 5, 9–10,
   34, 36, 61, 85, 91, 114
in effective teaching, 1
essential principles, 6–11
instructional procedures to
   maximize development of,
   3–4
language knowledge sources and,
   62
nature of literacy processing, 7
planning comprehensive literacy
   program, 113–119
reciprocal relationship between
   reading and writing, 8–9,
   93–94
research underlying, 1–3, 6
standards and, 9, 11, 32, 33, 61,
   62, 67, 71–72, 90, 94, 95,
   97–98, 104
success on steep gradient of
   difficulty, 10–11
teacher leadership in
   comprehensive change,
   113–119
writing with guidance and
   support, 95
Literal questions, 56
Lobel, A., 19
Lose, M. K., 38
Luck, M., 18, 20
Lyons, C. A., 16

MacArthur, C., 92–93
Malcolm, M., 50

Manyak, P. C., 110
Marie (student), 103–104
Marinak, B., 20
Mastre-O'Farrell, J., 110
Mathematics
    integrating writing instruction in,
        93–94
    math centers, 26
Matt (student), 79–87, 89, 93, 94
May, H., 1, 2, 11, 114
McCardle, P., 109
McCloskey, R., 107, 108
McCutcheon, D., 92–93
McGee, L. M., 44
McKay, R., 39, 41
McKeown, M. G., 109–110
McLaughlin, M., 22
McMaster, K. L., 64
McNamara, D. S., 64
McNaughton, S., 44
Measurement centers, 25
Meisinger, E. B., 106
Milk to Ice Cream (Snyder), 62
Miller, A. C., 63, 64
Miss Rumphius (Cooney), 52–54, 56,
    57–58
Monterey Bay Aquarium Live Web
    Cams, 73, 74
Morrison, F. J., 18, 20
Morris, R. D., 106
Morrow, L. M., 16, 18, 19, 20, 33, 45,
    54, 106
Moss, B., 64, 78, 86
Murphy, B., 7
Murphy, J. A., 2
Music, 70

Nagaoka, J. K., 26
Narrative text, 46–95. See also
    Informational texts
    Discussion Webs, 51, 58–59
    Experience-Text Relationship,
        57–58
    graphic organizers, 54, 55–56,

        76–77, 80–83
    guided retelling, 54–55
    integrated decoding and
        comprehension instruction,
        47–49, 50
    interactive read-aloud and teacher
        questioning, 51–54
    Readers Theatre, 54–55, 70, 73,
        74
    reading for enjoyment and
        understanding, 49–50
    story maps, 54, 55–56
    teaching for meaning and
        comprehension, 50–59
National Council of Teachers of
    English, 17
National Geographic, 73
National Geographic Kids, 74
National Geographic, Starfish, 74
National Geographic Windows in
    Literacy Early, 74
National Geographic Windows on
    Literacy Language, Literacy and
    Vocabulary, 74
National Governors Association
    Center for Best Practice
    (NGACBP), 9, 10, 26, 62, 90, 100
National Institute of Child Health
    and Human Development, 10, 18,
    50, 51
National Reading Panel, 10, 51
National Wildlife Foundation, 74, 76
Nelson, K. S., 44
Neuman, S. B., 63, 65
Newmann, F. M., 26
Next Generation Science Standards,
    67, 71

Observation Survey of Early Literacy
    Achievement, An (Clay, 2013), 26,
    27, 29, 32, 91, 104–105, 116
Observing Young Readers (Clay, 1982),
    3, 6, 32, 51
O'Leary, S., 109, 112

Olinghouse, N., 92–93
Olson, C. B., 92–93
One Morning in Maine (McCloskey), 107–108
Opitz, M. F., 26
Oral retelling, 70
Osborn, A. F., 90

Paired Reading activity, 24
Paired research activities, 75, 76–77
Parris, S. R., 18
Partner reading, 107
Partnership for 21st Century Skills, 61, 64
Partner talk, 48
Pearson, P. D., 3, 50, 51, 64, 65, 71
Philipp, R. A., 118
Phonemic awareness, 8, 36, 40, 85
Phonics, 32
Phonological awareness, 32
Piasta, S. B., 20
Pinkhorn, A., 63
Pinnell, G. S., 16, 20–21, 57, 101–104, 121–122
Polacco, Patricia, 49
Polar Bears (National Geographic Windows on Literacy Early), 74
"Polynesian Language Skills of Maori and Samoan School Entrants, The" (Clay, 1971), 3
Pratt, A., 17
Pressley, M., 16, 18, 19, 20, 33, 45, 51
Preventing Reading Difficulties (Snow et al.), 51
Prewriting processes, 90–91
    choice in, 90–91
    knowledge building in, 90
    rehearsal in, 91
Priebe, S. J., 63
Prior knowledge, 63
Problem-solving activities
    in running records, 27–29, 92
    in spelling, 81, 85–86, 87–89

in vocabulary development, 110
in working with sorts of information, 6, 61
writing as active problem solving, 79–85
Promising Literacy for Every Child (Askew et al.), 121–122
Prompting. *See* Teacher(s)
Punctuation, 39

Radio reading, 107
Rain Forest, The (National Geographic Windows in Literacy Early), 74
RAND Reading Study Group, 3
Ranger Rick, 65
Rapp, D. N., 64
Rasinski, R. V., 106
Read-aloud, 51–54, 69, 81
Readers Theatre (Sloyer), 54–55, 70, 73, 74
Reading
    accuracy scores, 1–2, 11, 29, 38, 46, 102–103, 105–106, 108, 111
    activities in units of study, 69
    alphabet books in, 42
    anticipating narrative text structure, 54–56
    basal reading programs, 52, 66, 100, 106–107
    choral, 70, 105, 107
    comprehension as key priority, 10, 59, 63
    conversations with children after reading new book, 57–58
    defined, 61
    Discussion Webs, 51, 58–59
    for enjoyment and understanding, 49–50
    guided, 20–21, 65, 69, 73
    independent, 21, 22, 25, 29, 36, 38, 47, 49, 69, 86, 98, 104, 105, 106, 111

Reading (*continued*)
  integrating decoding and
    comprehension instruction,
    47–49
  integrating writing instruction in,
    93–94
  interactive read-aloud and teacher
    questioning, 51–54
  in knowledge-building process,
    63–64
  reciprocal relationship with
    writing, 8–9, 93–94
  shared, 37–38, 39, 106–108
  small-group instruction in, 20–24,
    37–38
  strategic activity in, 49–50
  teacher introductions to new
    texts, 48–49
  teacher prompts for letter use in,
    42–44
  teaching for meaning and
    comprehension, 50–59
  text complexity levels in, 100–106
Reading (Clay, 1979), 2
Reading Recovery (Clay, 1993), 2, 3
Reading Recovery®
  development of, 1–3
  differentiated instruction in,
    16–17
  for grade 1, failing readers only, 2
  research and theory development
    underlying, 1–3, 6, 114
Reading Workshop, 93
Reed, K. L., 18
Rehearsal, in writing informational
  texts, 91
Rereading strategy, 28, 37–38, 47–48,
  105
Research, 75–77
  modeling how to locate
    information, 76–77
  preparing students for, 75–76
Reteaching, 35
Retelling, 54–55, 70

Reutzel, D. R., 39, 40, 106
Robb, L., 50, 102
Ross, G., 48
Ross, K., 50
Ross, P., 14, 118, 119
Rothenberg, C., 91
"Round-robin" reading, 14, 22–24
Running record assessment, 27–29,
  31, 33, 44–45, 91–92, 104–105,
  116
*Running Records for Classroom
  Teachers* (Clay, 2000a), 27, 29, 31,
  104–105, 116

Savage, R. S., 7
Scaffolding, 48, 50, 59, 75, 77, 78,
  86, 117
Scanlon, D. M., 17
Scarcella, R., 108, 110
Schappelle, B. P., 118
Scharer, P. L., 121–122
Schatschneider, C., 17, 18, 20, 50
Schmitt, M. C., 16
Schwanenflugel, P. J., 106
Schwartz, R. M., 2, 31, 43
Science centers, 26
Searfoss, L., 107
Self-confidence, and "round-robin"
  reading, 23
Self-correcting strategy, 7, 8, 28–29,
  51, 102, 104
Self-esteem, and "round-robin"
  reading, 23
Self-monitoring strategy, 28–29, 102,
  104
Semantics, 8
Sequence words, 54
Shanahan, T., 50, 108, 109, 110
Shared reading
  in fluency oriented reading
    instruction (FORI), 106–108
  in teaching concepts about print,
    37–38, 39
Siamon, S., 36

Sipay, E. R., 17
Sirinides, P., 1, 2, 11, 114
Slowik, H. Y., 32
Sloyer, S., 54–55, 70
Small-group instruction, 20–26
    eliminating "round-robin"
        reading, 14, 22–24
    focused teaching in, 20
    heterogeneous groups in, 24
    homogeneous groups in, 20–22
    independent reading in, 22
    interest-based groups, 24
    shared reading time in, 37–38
    short time frame for, 20
    units of study, 73–74
    work-time activities or centers
        and, 25–26
Small, S. G., 17
Smolkin, L. B., 84
Snow, C. E., 51
Snowling, M. J., 17
Snyder, I., 62
Social studies, integrating writing
    instruction in, 93–94
Soffos, C., 93
Sparks, S. D., 2
Speaking, activities in units of study,
    70
Spelling strategies
    systematic observation, 29–30, 31
    in writing informational texts, 81,
        85–86, 87–89
Stahl, S. A., 106–108
Starfish (Hurd), 73, 74
Stauffer, R. G., 69
Storybook reading, 37
Story maps, 54, 55–56
Strachan, S. L., 65
Strategic activity
    for comprehension, 50–59
    defined, 5, 49
    importance to students, 4–6, 7
    in reading, 49–50
    rereading, 28, 37–38, 47–48, 105

self-correction, 7, 8, 28–29, 51,
    102, 104
self-monitoring, 28–29, 102, 104
spelling, 81, 85–86, 87–89
Strategic change, teacher leadership
    in, 113–119
Struggling readers and writers, 16,
    17, 24, 70, 115, 116
Sulzby, E., 86
Summative assessment, 72
Syntactic information, 8
Systematic observation, 26–30
    as basis of instructional decisions,
        30
    running record assessment, 27–29,
        33, 44–45, 91–92, 104–105
    spelling, 29–30, 31
    and teacher leadership in
        comprehensive change, 118
    in writing informational texts,
        91–92

Taba, H., 90
Taft, M. L., 64
Take-home reading, 107
Targeted instructional solutions,
    16–17
Tasks with scope, 26
Taxonomy of Educational Objectives
    (Bloom & Krathwohl), 56
Taylor, B. M., 51
Teacher(s). See also Teacher
    leadership
    characteristics of exemplary, 16,
        19, 20, 30, 33, 51, 114, 119
    collaborative relationships with
        other professionals, 1, 67,
        80–85, 119–121
    conversations with children after
        reading new book, 57–58
    demonstrating concepts about
        print, 38, 41
    with "encompassing commitment
        to thoughtful practice," 1

Teacher(s) (*continued*)
    exemplary, 16, 19, 20, 30, 33, 51,
        114, 119
    instructional scaffolding by, 48,
        50, 59, 75, 77, 78, 86, 117
    introductions to new texts, 48–49
    minimizing "teacher talk," 20, 34,
        38, 39
    modeling how to locate
        information, 76–77
    prompting for children's use of
        print, 38, 42–44
    prompting for children's use of
        sources of information, 51
    prompting while children write,
        86–89
    systematic observation by, 26–30
Teacher leadership
    collaborative extended learning
        through classroom teaching,
        119–121
    planning comprehensive literacy
        program, 113–119
Teacher questioning
    effective use in comprehension
        instruction, 56–59
    interactive read-aloud and, 51–54
    "known-answer" questions in, 56
    question types, 56–57
"Teaching Essential Vocabulary
    to English Language Learners"
    (O'Leary), 112
Teale, W. H., 39, 41
Templeton, S., 29
Text complexity levels, 100–106
    complex text, 100
    easy text, 106
    familiar text, 105
    frustration level text, 100–102
    instructional level text, 102–105
Tharp, R., 57–58
Think-aloud, 81
Thinking cards, 97–98

Thomas (teacher), 97–100, 102–104,
    109–110
Thompson, L. A., 7
Thomson, S. L., 74
Three-columned charts, 80, 81
Three-sentence writing tasks, 80–82
Tiu, R. D., 7
Topping, K., 24
Torgesen, J., 50
Tracey, D. H., 18
Trail of Tears, The (Bruchac), 97–100,
    102–104, 109–110
Tunmer, W. E., 7
26 Letters and 99 Cents (Hoban), 42

Underwood, P. S., 18, 20
U.S. Department of Education, 2,
    92–93, 120
Units of study, 66–77
    activities in, 69–71, 73, 75
    analyzing quality of unit resource
        and activities, 71, 72, 74
    balancing activities, 70–71
    content areas, 67, 68
    creating tasks and activities,
        69–70
    culminating activities, 75
    essential questions, 67, 68
    goals of, 66
    grade-appropriate collaborative
        research, 75–77
    implementing, 73
    material selection, 68–69
    planning, 67–69
    rationale for, 66–67
    sample "Habitat" unit, 71–75
    scope, 67, 68
    sequencing activities, 70
    standards and objectives in, 67–68
    and teacher leadership in
        comprehensive change, 119
    theme selection, 67, 68
    unit assessment, 71

Valencia, S. W., 3, 71
Van den Broek, P., 64
Van Sluys, K., 100
Vellutino, F. R., 17
Vocabulary instruction, 64, 108–111
Vocabulary notebooks, 73
Von Gunten, H., 110

Walker-Dalhouse, D., 20
Walpole, S., 51
Watson, B., 86
Watts-Taffe, S., 20
Wharton-MacDonald, R., 16, 19, 20, 33, 45
Wharton-McDonald, C., 51
"What Did I Write?" (Clay, 1975), 7
What Lives in a Tide Pool (National Geographic Windows in Literacy Early), 74
What Works Clearinghouse (U.S. Department of Education), 92–93, 120
Whiteboards, 5, 34, 35, 41, 47, 52–53, 90
Whitely, C. S., 18
Whittaker, D., 90
Whole-class instruction
    letter/word knowledge in, 39–44
    minimizing, 18–20
    shared reading time in, 37–38
    short time frame for, 20
    units of study, 66–77
    writing informational texts, 79–85
Williams, J. L., 10
Wixson, K., 3, 71
Wold, J., 116
Wood, D., 48
Woo, D. G., 18, 106
Word recognition, 32
World Wildlife Fund, 74
Wright, W. E., 24

Writing. *See also* Writing informational texts
    activities in units of study, 69–70
    couplets, 84–85
    independent, 79, 81–83, 86, 94, 95
    in letter/word knowledge, 41–42
    reciprocal relationship with reading, 8–9, 93–94
    three-sentence writing tasks, 80–82
    vocabulary development for English language learners (ELLs), 108–111
Writing centers, 25
Writing informational texts, 69–70, 79–95
    comparison of literacy processing theories and California Common Core State Standards, 95
    dedicated time for writing, 92–94
    guided support in, 85–87
    integration within subject areas, 93–94
    lesson examples, 79–85, 94
    prewriting processes, 90–91
    spelling strategies, 81, 85–86, 87–89
    systematic observation by teacher, 91–92
    writing as active problem-solving, 79–85
    writing strategies in, 87–89, 94
Writing strategies, 87–89, 94
Writing Workshop, 93

Yancey, K. B., 89–90
Young, T. A., 86

Zhang, H., 17

About the Authors

Sharan A. Gibson, PhD, is professor emeritus of literacy education at San Diego State University. She served as graduate advisor for the MA in reading and reading specialist credential programs at SDSU, and director of the SDSU Community Reading Clinic. Sharan has worked in Reading Recovery® since 1992, is a member of the North American Trainers Group, and served as trainer of teacher leaders and director of the SDSU Reading Recovery program, lead editor of *Literacy Teaching and Learning*, and section editor of the *Journal of Reading Recovery*. Her research is focused on Reading Recovery teacher expertise, teachers' professional noticing ability, literacy coaching, and children's writing development and instruction. Sharan has also served as classroom teacher, mentor teacher, reading specialist, Reading Recovery teacher and teacher leader, early literacy consultant, and classroom literacy coach. She has published numerous articles and presents at local, state, and national conferences.

Barbara Moss, PhD, is professor emeritus of literacy education at San Diego State University. She has worked as an English language arts teacher at the middle and high school levels, a reading specialist in grades 3–9, and as a reading supervisor in a county office. She has been a university professor for the past 20 years. Her research interests are focused on teaching informational texts to all students, especially English learners. She has written widely about this topic, and is the author of more than 100 articles, columns, and book chapters. Her work has been published in *The Reading Teacher, The Journal of Literacy Research, Reading Psychology*, and numerous other journals. She has done hundreds of professional presentations nationally and internationally at conferences, teacher inservices, and teacher workshops. Her most recently published coauthored books include *A Close Look at Close Reading: Teaching Students to Analyze Complex Texts Grades K–5* (with Diane Lapp, Maria Grant, and Kelly Johnson) and *40 Strategies for Guiding Children Through Informational Texts* (with Virginia Loh-Hagan).